## DATE DUE

OCT 16

NOV 2 5 2014

CONSTITUTIONAL
AMENDMENTS
BEYOND THE BILL OF RIGHTS

# Amendment XIV
# Equal Protection

# Other Books of Related Interest

**Opposing Viewpoints Series**

Civil Liberties

Feminism

Race Relations

Work

Working Women

**Current Controversies Series**

Civil Liberties

Extremist Groups

Feminism

Human Rights

**CONSTITUTIONAL AMENDMENTS**
BEYOND THE BILL OF RIGHTS

# Amendment XIV
# Equal Protection

*Sylvia Engdahl, Book Editor*

**GREENHAVEN PRESS**
*A part of Gale, Cengage Learning*

**GALE**
CENGAGE Learning

Detroit • New York • San Francisco • New Haven, Conn • Waterville, Maine • London

GALE
CENGAGE Learning

© 2009 Greenhaven Press, a part of Gale, Cengage Learning.

Gale and Greenhaven Press are registered trademarks used herein under license.

*For more information, contact:*
Greenhaven Press
27500 Drake Rd.
Farmington Hills, MI 48331-3535
Or you can visit our Internet site at gale.cengage.com

For product information and technology assistance, contact us at

Gale Customer Support, 1-800-877-4253
For permission to use material from this text or product, submit all requests online at www.cengage.com/permissions

Further permissions questions can be emailed to permissionrequest@cengage.com

Articles in Greenhaven Press anthologies are often edited for length to meet page requirements. In addition, original titles of these works are changed to clearly present the main thesis and to explicitly indicate the author's opinion. Every effort is made to ensure that Greenhaven Press accurately reflects the original intent of the authors. Every effort has been made to trace the owners of copyrighted material.

Cover photograph © Bettmann/Corbis.

**LIBRARY OF CONGRESS CATALOGING-IN-PUBLICATION DATA**

Amendment XIV : equal protection / Sylvia Engdahl, book editor.
    p. cm. -- (Constitutional amendments: beyond the Bill of Rights)
    Includes bibliographical references and index.
    ISBN 978-0-7377-4126-1 (hardcover)
    1. Discrimination--Law and legislation--United States. 2. United States. Constitution. 14th Amendment. 3. Equality before the law--United States. 4. Minorities--Civil rights-- United States. 5. Immigrants--Civil rights--United States. I. Engdahl, Sylvia. II. Title: Amendment 14. III. Title: Amendment Fourteen.
    KF4755. A94 2009
    342.7308'5--dc22

                                                                    2008041006

Printed in the United States of America
2 3 4 5 6 7 12 11 10

# Contents

## Chapter 1: Historical Background of the Fourteenth Amendment

A congressman argues against the proposed constitutional amendment on the grounds that it would take away the right of the states to make their own laws, correctly foreseeing—as few did before the mid-twentieth century—that equal protection would lead to interracial marriage, the eligibility of blacks for the presidency, and the desegregation of schools.

One of the chief backers of the Fourteenth Amendment speaks on the floor of the House of Representatives to call for a vote on the bill as modified by the Senate, saying that although he is not satisfied with the proposition, he believes that it should be adopted without further delay to stave off further opposition.

In a speech on the importance of the Fourteenth Amendment to the future of the nation, a congressman comments on its first section, declaring that the Due Process and Equal Protection clauses "will be a jewel of beauty when placed in the Constitution of the country."

## Chapter 3: Equal Protection for Women, Immigrants, and Gays

## Chapter 4: Current Debate on Equal Protection

## Appendices

# Equal Protection

> *"Today's Constitution is a realistic document of freedom only because of several corrective amendments. Those amendments speak to a sense of decency and fairness."*
>
> *Thurgood Marshall*

While the U.S. Constitution forms the backbone of American democracy, the amendments make the Constitution a living, ever-evolving document. Interpretation and analysis of the Constitution inform lively debate in every branch of government, as well as among students, scholars, and all other citizens, and views on various articles of the Constitution have changed over the generations. Formally altering the Constitution, however, can happen only through the amendment process. The Greenhaven Press series The Bill of Rights examines the first ten amendments to the Constitution. Constitutional Amendments: Beyond the Bill of Rights continues the exploration, addressing key amendments ratified since 1791.

The process of amending the Constitution is painstaking. While other options are available, the method used for nearly every amendment begins with a congressional bill that must pass both the Senate and the House of Representatives by a two-thirds majority. Then the amendment must be ratified by three-quarters of the states. Many amendments have been proposed since the Bill of Rights was adopted in 1791, but only seventeen have been ratified.

It may be difficult to imagine a United States where women and African Americans are prohibited from voting, where the federal government allows one human being to enslave another, or where some citizens are denied equal protection under the law. While many of our most fundamental liberties are protected by the Bill of Rights, the amendments that followed have significantly broadened and enhanced the rights of American citizens. Such rights may be taken for granted today, but when the amendments were ratified, many were considered groundbreaking and proved to be explosively controversial.

Each volume in Constitutional Amendments provides an in-depth exploration of an amendment and its impact through primary and secondary sources, both historical and contemporary. Primary sources include landmark Supreme Court rulings, speeches by prominent experts, and newspaper editorials. Secondary sources include historical analyses, law journal articles, book excerpts, and magazine articles. Each volume first presents the historical background of the amendment, creating a colorful picture of the circumstances surrounding the amendment's passage: the campaigns to sway public opinion, the congressional debates, and the struggle for ratification. Next, each volume examines the ways the court system has been used to test the validity of the amendment and addresses the ramifications of the amendment's passage. The final chapter of each volume presents viewpoints that explore current controversies and debates relating to ways in which the amendment affects our everyday lives.

Numerous features are included in each Constitutional Amendments volume:

- An originally written introduction presents a concise yet thorough overview of the amendment.

- A time line provides historical context by describing key events, organizations, and people relating to the ratification of the amendment, subsequent court cases, and the impact of the amendment.

- An annotated table of contents offers an at-a-glance summary of each primary and secondary source essay included in the volume.

- The complete text of the amendment, followed by a "plain English" explanation, brings the amendment into clear focus for students and other readers.

- Graphs, charts, tables, and maps enhance the text.

- A list of all twenty-seven Constitutional Amendments offers quick reference.

- An annotated list of court cases relevant to the amendment broadens the reader's understanding of the judiciary's role in interpreting the Constitution.

- A bibliography of books, periodicals, and Web sites aids readers in further research.

- A detailed subject index allows readers to quickly find the information they need.

With the aid of this series, students and other researchers will become better informed of their rights and responsibilities as American citizens. Constitutional Amendments: Beyond the Bill of Rights examines the roots of American democracy, bringing to life the ways the Constitution has evolved and how it has impacted this nation's history.

# Amendment Text and Explanation

## The Fourteenth Amendment to the United States Constitution

*Passed by Congress June 13, 1866. Ratified July 9, 1868.*

Note: Article I, section 2, of the Constitution was modified by section 2 of the 14th amendment.

Section 1. All persons born or naturalized in the United States, and subject to the jurisdiction thereof, are citizens of the United States and of the State wherein they reside. No State shall make or enforce any law which shall abridge the privileges or immunities of citizens of the United States; nor shall any State deprive any person of life, liberty, or property, without due process of law; nor deny to any person within its jurisdiction the equal protection of the laws.

Section 2. Representatives shall be apportioned among the several States according to their respective numbers, counting the whole number of persons in each State, excluding Indians not taxed. But when the right to vote at any election for the choice of electors for President and Vice-President of the United States, Representatives in Congress, the Executive and Judicial officers of a State, or the members of the Legislature thereof, is denied to any of the male inhabitants of such State, being twenty-one years of age,* and citizens of the United States, or in any way abridged, except for participation in rebellion, or other crime, the basis of representation therein shall be reduced in the proportion which the number of such male citizens shall bear to the whole number of male citizens twenty-one years of age in such State.

Section 3. No person shall be a Senator or Representative in Congress, or elector of President and Vice-President, or

* *Changed by section 1 of the 26th amendment.*

hold any office, civil or military, under the United States, or under any State, who, having previously taken an oath, as a member of Congress, or as an officer of the United States, or as a member of any State legislature, or as an executive or judicial officer of any State, to support the Constitution of the United States, shall have engaged in insurrection or rebellion against the same, or given aid or comfort to the enemies thereof. But Congress may by a vote of two-thirds of each House, remove such disability.

Section 4. The validity of the public debt of the United States, authorized by law, including debts incurred for payment of pensions and bounties for services in suppressing insurrection or rebellion, shall not be questioned. But neither the United States nor any State shall assume or pay any debt or obligation incurred in aid of insurrection or rebellion against the United States, or any claim for the loss or emancipation of any slave; but all such debts, obligations and claims shall be held illegal and void.

Section 5. The Congress shall have the power to enforce, by appropriate legislation, the provisions of this article.

## Explanation

Section 1. Everyone who is born or naturalized in the United States, except members of Indian tribes and the children of foreign diplomats, is a citizen both of the United States and of the state in which he or she lives. (The exception for Indians was overridden by a law passed in 1924.) No state can make or enforce any law that abridges the privileges or immunities of U.S. citizens. (Exactly which privileges and immunities this covers has been controversial.) No state can deprive any person—not merely any citizen—of life, liberty, or property except through procedures established by law. Everyone within a state, not only its citizens, must be treated equally by its laws, without arbitrary discrimination.

Section 2. The number of a state's congressional representatives depends on the total population of the state, not counting Indians who are not taxed. However, if the right to vote in an election for federal or state office is denied to any male citizens over the age of twenty-one (changed by the twenty-sixth amendment to age eighteen) for any reason other than conviction of a crime, the number of that state's representatives will be proportionately reduced. (This provision was intended to penalize Southern states if they did not allow blacks to vote.)

Section 3. No one who has previously taken an oath to support the Constitution of the United States as a federal or state official is eligible to hold such an office, either civilian or military, after he or she has participated in an insurrection or [armed] rebellion against the United States, or has given aid to its enemies. However, Congress can make exceptions for individuals by a two-thirds vote. (This provision was intended to prevent officials of the Southern states who fought against the Union in the Civil War from holding office or military command in the future, unless they were individually permitted to do so by Congress.)

Section 4. The federal government must pay all its debts, including benefits owed to members of the Union Army or civilians who performed services during the war. However, neither the federal government nor any state government is allowed to pay any debt incurred by the defeated Confederacy, or any claims made by former slaveowners to be compensated for the loss of their slaves. (The Confederate states had borrowed money from foreign banks during the war; this clause states that those loans will not be repaid.)

Section 5. Congress shall have the power to pass laws to enforce all the above provisions.

*Because the Fourteenth Amendment has many distinct provisions, no single book in this series can cover all of them. This book covers only the Equal Protection Clause—that is, the last clause of Section 1.*

# Introduction

The Fourteenth Amendment brought about a fundamental change in the government of America. It is the most sweeping of the U.S. Constitution's amendments, and in fact, some scholars have called it "the second Constitution." The amendment's first section, which among other provisions ensures that all Americans have equal protection under state and local laws, has become a guarantee of civil rights for everyone.

It is now often forgotten that this guarantee did not always exist. At the time the United States was founded, the nation had no authority over how citizens were treated by state governments. It was a union of independent states, just as its name implies. The original Constitution, including the Bill of Rights (the first ten amendments), was concerned solely with what the federal government could and could not do. The states gave citizens only those rights that their individual constitutions or legislatures chose to specify.

During the first half of the nineteenth century, there was increasing concern over the differences among what individual states did. The most serious conflict was over slavery. The Southern states had from the beginning insisted on allowing ownership of slaves, on which their economy depended, while Northerners opposed slavery on moral grounds. There was much bitterness on both sides over whether border states and new states would permit it. Eventually, when the Southern states seceded from the Union and the other states determined to preserve it as a single nation, this dispute erupted into the long and bloody Civil War.

After the war, Congress was faced with the problem of how to restore the South and bring the Southern states back into the Union. First by the Emancipation Proclamation of President Abraham Lincoln and later by the Thirteenth Amendment to the U.S. Constitution, the slaves were set free.

But blacks in the South still did not have any civil rights. The Southern states had no intention of giving them the same rights as whites; but the Northerners, who had total control of Congress because no representatives of the defeated states had yet been readmitted, considered justice for blacks—for which many had fought and died—absolutely essential.

Today, most Americans think of "equal rights" as meaning minority rights. But in many parts of South at the time of the Civil War, blacks were not a minority. They were a majority in three states and in some congressional districts of the others, for there had been a great many slaves. That was one reason why giving blacks equal rights, and especially the right to vote, was resisted by Southern whites—it meant that they would be in the minority themselves and that their leaders might well be voted out of office. Freed blacks could hardly be expected to pass laws favorable to their former masters. Furthermore, because it had been against the law to teach slaves to read and write, nearly all of them were uneducated. So Southern whites fostered the idea that blacks were inferior in order to prevent their governments from being taken over by them, and they passed laws known as the Black Codes to restrict their rights.

In an attempt to override the Black Codes, Congress passed the Civil Rights Act of 1866. However, there was some doubt as to whether it had the authority to do so (that law is still in effect, and in May 2008, the Supreme Court decided a case on the basis of it). Congress therefore realized that only a constitutional amendment could enable it to regulate the actions of the states, and the congressional committee in charge of postwar reconstruction began work on what became the Fourteenth Amendment. Its main author was John Bingham, a representative of Ohio, who had long had a vision of an ideal republic in which everyone would be equal; he said, "The equality of all to the right to live; the right to know; to argue and to utter, according to conscience; to work and enjoy the product of their toil, is the rock on which [the] Constitution rests, its sure foundation and defense." It was he who was chiefly responsible for the new amendment's first section. There was little opposition in Congress to that section on principle, although a few members foresaw that placing it in the Constitution might eventually lead to broader rights for blacks than most people of that era could ever imagine. However, some Northerners objected to the Equal Protection Clause for a different reason: They did not believe the federal government should be given the power to override state laws.

Debating a draft of the amendment, Robert S. Hale, a representative of New York, protested that it was "a grant of the fullest and most ample power to Congress" to make all laws necessary to protect the rights of all persons in all the states "with the simple proviso that such protection shall be equal." Was this not "introducing a power never before intended to be conferred upon Congress? For all we know it is true that probably every state in the Union fails to give equal protection to all persons within its borders in the rights of life, liberty and property. . . . It may be a fault in the States that they do not do it. A reformation may be desirable, but . . . reforms of this nature should come from the States, and not be forced upon them by the centralized power of the Federal Government."

To take an example, he continued, "There is not to-day a State in the Union where there is not a distinction between the rights of married women, as to property, and the rights of *femmes sole* [single women] and men." In answer to the argument that perhaps the Equal Protection Clause meant only that no distinction was to be made between two married women, or between two single women, he pointed out that by such reasoning, "it will be sufficient if you extend to one negro the same rights you do to another, but not those you extend to a white man." Thus, that could not be the intended interpretation, though no one seriously thought that the amendment might someday lead to equal rights for women.

Hale went on to say that the wording of the existing Constitution should be compared with "what I cannot but characterize, with all my respect and deference for the committee on reconstruction, as the extremely vague, loose, and indefinite provisions of the proposed amendment.... You will find no general power granted to Congress [by the original Constitution] to legislate upon matters of a municipal nature, or matters relating to the social or civil rights of citizens of the States, but everywhere it points most strictly and carefully to the legitimate objects for which the national Government was created."

An editorial in the *New York Times*, commenting on Hale's speech, said, "He regards [the Equal Protection Clause] as a wide and dangerous departure from the fundamental principles of Government.... He supports this view with an argument of great clearness and force... The amendment seems to be only another of the steps proposed by the radicals in Congress for a consolidation of the central power and the complete overthrow of State authority." Despite his reservations Hale voted in favor of the amendment's final version, which was passed by a large margin. To most members of Congress, its first section meant only what they wanted it to mean, which was the elimination of Southern laws that restricted blacks, and the majority did not worry too much about possible future interpretations. Yet Hale's prediction proved to be correct. Not only did the amendment give unprecedented power to the federal government, but its wording was indeed vague—the Supreme Court has been arguing ever since about what it implies.

Only five years after ratification of the Fourteenth Amendment, the Court interpreted the Equal Protection Clause for the first time in a group of 1873 cases known as the Slaughterhouse Cases. Holding that a group of Louisiana butchers could not rely on the clause to challenge a state monopoly, the Court wrote, "We doubt very much whether any action of a

State not directed by way of discrimination against the negroes as a class, or on account of their race, will ever be held to come within the purview of this provision." However, three years later, in *Yick Wo v. Hopkins*, the Court ruled that the Equal Protection Clause applied to all persons, including Chinese immigrants, who at that time were not allowed to become U.S. citizens. That clause was not used to achieve equality of rights between men and women until much later; not until 1971 did the Supreme Court first rule that discrimination against women was a violation of equal protection. State laws that discriminate against gays were not held to be unconstitutional until 1996.

Meanwhile, the extent of the rights protected, as well as the classifications of people protected, has been expanded gradually. Although at least one member of Congress argued in the debates leading to adoption of the amendment that "equal protection" would mean that blacks and whites must be allowed to attend the same schools and to intermarry, this did not happen in the Southern states for a long time. In 1896, in *Plessy v. Ferguson*, the Supreme Court held that racial segregation was constitutional as long as accommodations were equal. This ruling was not overturned until 1954, when segregated schools were ruled unconstitutional under the Equal Protection Clause. It was nearly a hundred years, from ratification of the Fourteenth Amendment in 1868 until 1967, before laws against racial intermarriage was declared unconstitutional.

These delays, which seem strange today, were attributable to the fact that the clause was interpreted according to what its authors were presumed to have intended when they wrote it, considering the customs of the society that existed in their era. Some legal experts believe that this is the way all law should be interpreted. Others believe that it should be interpreted in light of modern conditions, and increasingly, that view has prevailed.

It is important to realize that what the Equal Protection Clause ensures is simply that everyone in a given state will have the same rights—or will lack the same rights, if no other provision of the Constitution guarantees them. A liberty that does not exist for anyone in a state cannot be claimed under the Equal Protection Clause (although under the Due Process Clause, it may). By now, it has been ruled that the Fourteenth Amendment makes the Bill of Rights applicable to state and local governments as well as to the federal government, but this was not always the case. The question of whether Congress intended the Fourteenth Amendment to incorporate the Bill of Rights has been controversial, though it is known that John Bingham did; and so this has happened slowly, a few rights at a time.

Another limitation of the Fourteenth Amendment—and thus of the Equal Protection Clause—is that it applies only to state and local governments, not to the federal government or to the actions of private organizations. It says "no State shall," and that is literally what it means. Actions of the federal government can also be found unconstitutional, but only under other articles of the Constitution. For example, when federal laws or regulations are held to deny equal protection, it is under the Fifth Amendment, not the Fourteenth, that they are ruled illegal.

Despite the early cases in which the Equal Protection Clause of the Fourteenth Amendment was cited for reasons not connected with racial issues, it was not often used as the basis for Supreme Court decisions until the 1960s. Since that time it has become increasingly important as a means of ensuring justice for all Americans.

# Chronology

## 1863

On January 1 President Abraham Lincoln issues the Emancipation Proclamation, declaring that "all persons held as slaves" within the rebellious states "are, and henceforward shall be free." This applies only to the Confederate states; slaves in border states are unaffected. The proclamation also gives blacks the right to serve in the Union army and navy.

## 1865

On January 31 the Thirteenth Amendment, ending slavery in the United States, is proposed by Congress.

On April 9 the Civil War ends with the surrender of General Robert E. Lee to the Union commander, Ulysses S. Grant.

On April 14 Abraham Lincoln is assassinated. Vice President Andrew Johnson, who was elected on the National Union Party ticket because of support from the faction of Democrats who had favored the war, becomes president. He soon clashes with the Republicans, who control Congress.

On December 6 the Thirteenth Amendment is ratified by the states and goes into effect.

In December Congress appoints the Committee on Reconstruction, consisting of nine members from the House of Representatives and six members from the Senate, to decide first, under what conditions the Southern states will be readmitted to the Union, and second, the status of blacks under the law.

## 1866

In March Congress passes a civil rights bill intended to counter the Black Codes in effect in the Southern states, which restrict the rights of blacks. This bill makes it a federal crime to deprive any person of civil rights. The bill is vetoed by President

Andrew Johnson, who opposes giving power to the federal government and argues that blacks are not qualified to become citizens.

Also in March the Committee on Reconstruction submits to Congress a draft, authored primarily by Ohio congressman John Bingham, of what is to become the Fourteenth Amendment. After debate, it is adopted by the House and sent to the Senate, which sends it back to the committee for revision.

On April 9 Congress passes the Civil Rights Act over the president's veto. This bill declares that "all persons born in the United States and not subject to any foreign power, excluding Indians not taxed," are citizens of the United States, "without regard to any previous condition of slavery or involuntary servitude."

On June 13 Congress passes a bill proposing the final version of the Fourteenth Amendment for ratification. The fall congressional elections are seen as a national referendum on it. During the year, it is ratified by six states.

## 1867

On March 2 Congress passes—over President Johnson's veto—the first of four Reconstruction Acts, giving the vote to blacks and providing, among other things, that all Southern states must ratify the Fourteenth Amendment in order to be readmitted to the Union.

During the year, the Fourteenth Amendment is ratified by sixteen states.

## 1868

Five more states ratify the Fourteenth Amendment. On July 9 it is ratified by the twenty-eighth state, the last needed for it to become law. However, two states attempt to rescind their ratification (Ohio and New Jersey), and there is uncertainty as to whether the rescissions are effective. On July 20 Secretary of State William H. Seward issues a proclamation certifying that it will become part of the U.S. Constitution if they are not. By July 28, after two additional states have ratified the amendment, Seward certifies unconditionally that it is in effect.

## 1869

On February 26 Congress proposes the Fifteenth Amendment, giving blacks the right to vote.

On March 4 Ulysses S. Grant becomes president.

## 1870

On February 3, ratification of the Fifteenth Amendment is completed.

On May 31 Congress passes "An Act to enforce the Right of Citizens of the United States to vote in the several States of this Union." It also contains provisions for enforcing the Fourteenth Amendment and reenacts the Civil Rights Act of 1866.

## 1871

On April 20, after long debate, Congress passes "An Act to enforce the Provisions of the Fourteenth Amendment to the Constitution of the United States," known variously as the Enforcement Act, the Ku Klux Klan Act, or the Civil Rights Act of 1871. It allows President Grant to send federal troops to enforce the law. This is needed because the Ku Klux Klan, a white supremacist organization, has been using violent terrorist tactics against blacks and Southern whites who support them. However, its opponents believe that it gives the federal government too much power.

## 1873

In a series of cases known as the Slaughterhouse Cases involving the rights of independent butchers versus a monopoly of slaughterhouse owners, the Supreme Court interprets the Fourteenth Amendment for the first time and rules, among other things, that it was intended only to protect the rights of former slaves, disallowing a broader interpretation.

## 1875

On March 1 Congress enacts the Civil Rights Act of 1875, which provides that "all persons within the jurisdiction of the United States shall be entitled to the full and equal and enjoyment of the accommodations, advantages, facilities, and privileges of inns, public conveyances on land or water, theaters, and other places of public amusement." It is rarely enforced.

The Supreme Court rules unanimously in *United States v. Cruikshank* that the Equal Protection Clause applies only to state actions, not to the actions of one citizen against another.

## 1880

In *Strauder v. West Virginia* the Supreme Court rules that to exclude blacks from juries violates the equal protection right of black criminal defendants.

## 1883

In the Civil Rights Cases the Supreme Court rules that the Civil Rights Act of 1875 is unconstitutional because the Fourteenth Amendment prohibits discrimination by states, not individuals, and Congress has no power to regulate the conduct of private companies. This decision severely limits the power of the federal government to protect the rights of blacks.

## 1886

In *Yick Wo v. Hopkins* the Supreme Court rules that laws that effectively discriminate against a particular group—in this case, the Chinese—are unconstitutional. This is the first time the Equal Protection Clause is applied to a minority other than blacks.

## 1896

In the landmark case *Plessy v. Ferguson*, the Supreme Court rules that racial segregation is constitutional, thus establishing the "separate but equal" doctrine that remains in effect for more than half a century.

**1925**

In *Gitlow v. New York* the Supreme Court rules that the Fourteenth Amendment extends some provisions of the Bill of Rights—namely, freedom speech and freedom of the press—to state governments, whereas previously they had applied only to the federal government. Later, this ruling becomes a precedent for extending other provisions of the Bill of Rights to the states.

**1938**

In *Missouri ex rel. Gaines v. Canada*, the first case to consider equality of education for blacks, the Supreme Court rules that if a state provides legal education for white students, it must also provide it to black students, and if the state has only one law school, blacks must be admitted.

In *United States v. Carolene Products* the idea of requiring different levels of scrutiny for different types of equal protection cases is first proposed. Since then, "strict scrutiny" has been used in cases involving fundamental rights, such as First Amendment rights, or discrimination involving race or national origin; this requires that a law must be "narrowly tailored" to serve a "compelling" government interest, and there must be no "less restrictive" means available for achieving the same result. In most other cases, only a "rational basis" test is needed, meaning that a law is constitutional if it is "reasonably related" to a "legitimate" government interest.

**1944**

In *Smith v. Allwright* the Supreme Court rules that people cannot be excluded from political parties on the basis of race. The Court holds that although parties are private organizations not normally covered by the Fourteenth Amendment, where one party is so dominant in a state as to determine the outcome of elections, a person who cannot vote in the primaries would be denied equal protection of the right to a meaningful vote.

## 1950

The Supreme Court rules in *McLaurin v. Oklahoma State Regents* that it is a violation of the Equal Protection Clause for a public institution of higher learning to treat a student differently solely because of his or her race.

## 1954

In the landmark case *Brown v. Board of Education*, the Supreme Court overturns *Plessy v. Ferguson* by ruling that racial segregation in public schools is unconstitutional under the Equal Protection Clause.

## 1962

The Supreme Court rules in *Baker v. Carr* that it is a violation of the Equal Protection Clause for lines between voting districts to be drawn in a way that gives some districts more people than others, thus making urban citizens' votes worth less than those of rural citizens. This decision requires reapportionment in many states and increases the political power of urban centers.

## 1967

In *Loving v. Virginia* the Supreme Court rules that under the Equal Protection Clause, laws against interracial marriage are unconstitutional.

## 1971

In *Reed v. Reed*, the first Supreme Court case in which the Equal Protection Clause is used to establish the rights of women, the Court rules that men cannot automatically be preferred over women as administrators of estates.

## 1976

In *Craig v. Boren* the Supreme Court rules for the first time that laws classifying people by gender must be subjected to "intermediate scrutiny," meaning that a law is unconstitutional under the Equal Protection Clause unless it is "substantially related" to an "important" government interest.

## 1982

The Supreme Court rules in *Plyler v. Doe* that the Fourteenth Amendment applies to all persons who reside in a state regardless of whether they are citizens, and therefore the children of illegal immigrants have a right to the same free education given other children.

## 1996

In *Romer v. Evans* the Supreme Court rules that under the Equal Protection Clause, states cannot prohibit local governments from passing ordinances to protect homosexuals from discrimination.

In *United States v. Virginia* the Supreme Court rules that gender-based restrictions on admission to a publicly supported school or college violate the Equal Protection Clause.

## 2000

The outcome of the presidential election is determined by the Supreme Court when in *Bush v. Gore* it rules that because Florida's standards for recounting ballots are inconsistent among counties, they do not provide voters with equal protection under the law, and therefore the recount must be stopped.

## 2003

In *Grutter v. Bollinger* the Supreme Court rules that using race as a factor in college admissions does not violate the constitutional right to equal protection if the policy is "narrowly tailored" to achieve racial diversity among the student body and the selection is made on an individual basis.

The Fourteenth Amendment is ratified by the last two states that were in the Union at the time of its adoption, New Jersey and Ohio, both of which had rescinded their original ratifications in 1868.

## 2007

In *Parents Involved in Community Schools v. Seattle School District*, the Supreme Court rules that it is a violation of the

Equal Protection Clause to use race as an arbitrary factor in assigning students to schools, even if the purpose is to maintain racial diversity. This decision is expected to have a significant effect on the "affirmative action" policies of many school districts.

CONSTITUTIONAL
AMENDMENTS
BEYOND THE BILL OF RIGHTS

CHAPTER 1

# Historical Background on the Fourteenth Amendment

# Speech in the House of Representatives Opposing Adoption of the Fourteenth Amendment

*Andrew Rogers*

*In the following excerpt from a speech made in the U.S. House of Representatives on February 26, 1866, Representative Andrew Rogers of New Jersey argues against the proposal to amend the Constitution that would later become the Fourteenth Amendment. Rogers strongly opposed amending the Constitution in any way that would interfere with the right of states to make their own laws. Like many men of his era, he believed that giving the federal government the power to override state laws would endanger the liberty of the people. However, his foresight as to what the Equal Protection Clause of the amendment would mean in practice was unusual. In this speech he points out that it would give blacks the right to become president, to marry whites, and to attend the same schools as whites—possibilities that most people of the time viewed as undesirable and did not take seriously. Many years passed before the Equal Protection Clause was interpreted as literally as Rogers predicted it might be. School segregation was not ruled unconstitutional until 1954, and state laws forbidding racial intermarriage were not ruled unconstitutional until 1967, more than a hundred years after Rogers recognized—albeit with disapproval—that this was what the Equal Protection Clause would require.*

*Andrew Rogers represented the state of New Jersey in Congress from 1863 to 1867.*

Andrew Rogers, U.S. House of Representatives, February 26, 1866. *Appendix to the Congressional Globe*, 39th Congress, pp. 133–35. http://lcweb2.loc.gov/ammem/amlaw/lwcg.html.

I had hoped, after what has transpired in the last few days, that the time had come when the Constitution of the United States would be secure from invasion by Congress. When I heard the words of the President of the United States in commendation of that sacred instrument, and as I rejoiced at the course pursued by conservative men on the other side of the House who are determined to sustain that instrument as it was given to us by our fathers, I had good reason to believe there would be no other amendments to it proposed by this body or the Senate. I felt that the agitation which had been kept up in this House against that instrument in order to amend it, as the President says, so that no more respect would be paid to it than to a mere resolution of a town meeting, had gone by, and that we would now dedicate the balance of our time in Congress to the great doctrine of constitutional liberty that we might give power to a free and patriotic President in his great work of reconstruction. . . .

## The Proposed Amendment Is Dangerous

I do think, notwithstanding the position which has been assumed by the eloquent and learned gentleman from Ohio [Mr. John Bingham] who reported this resolution, that no resolution proposing an amendment to the Constitution of the United States had been offered to this Congress more dangerous to the liberties of the people and the foundations of this Government than the pending resolution. When sifted from top to bottom it will be found to be the embodiment of centralization and the disfranchisement of the States of those sacred and immutable State rights which were reserved to them by the consent of our fathers in our organic law [the fundamental laws of the United States, including the Declaration of Independence, the Articles of Confederation, and the Constitution].

When the gentleman says the proposed amendment is intended to authorize no rights except those already embodied in the Constitution, I give him the plain and emphatic answer—if the Constitution provides the requirements contained in this amendment, why, in this time of excitement and public clamor, should we attempt to again ingraft upon it what is already in it?. . .

If those rights already exist in the organic law of the land, I ask him, what is the necessity of so amending the Constitution as to authorize Congress to carry into effect a plain provision which now, according to his views, inheres in the very organic law itself?

I know what the gentleman will attempt to say in answer to that position: that because the Constitution authorizes Congress to carry the powers conferred by it into effect, privileges and immunities are not considered within the meaning of powers, and therefore Congress has no right to carry into effect what the Constitution itself intended when it provided that citizens of each State should have all privileges and immunities of citizens in the several States.

## The Framers of the Constitution Did Not Intend Congress to Override State Laws

Now, sir, the answer to that argument is simply this: that when the Constitution was framed and ratified, its makers did not intend to lodge in the Congress of the United States any power to override a State and settle by congressional legislation the rights, privileges, and immunities of citizens in the several States. That matter was left entirely for the courts, to enforce the privileges and immunities of the citizens under that clause of the organic law. Although our forefathers, in their wisdom, after having exacted and wrested from Great Britain State rights, saw fit to incorporate in the Constitution such a principle in regard to citizens of the several States, yet they never intended to give to Congress the power, by virtue of that clause, to control the local domain of a State or the privileges and immunities of citizens in the State, even though they had come from another State. . . .

But this proposed amendment goes much further than the Constitution goes in the language which it uses with regard to the privileges and immunities of citizens in the several States. It proposes so to amend it that all persons in the several States shall by act of Congress have equal protection in regard to life, liberty, and property. If the bill to protect all persons in the United States in their civil rights and furnish the means of their vindication, which has just passed the Senate by almost the entire vote of the Republican party be constitutional, what, I ask, is the use of this proposed amendment? What is the use of authorizing Congress to do more than Congress has already done, so far as one branch is concerned, in passing a bill to guaranty civil rights and immunities to the people of the United States without distinction of race or color? If it is necessary now to amend the Constitution of the United States in the manner in which the learned gentleman who reported this amendment proclaims, then the vote of the Senate of the United States in passing that bill guarantying civil rights to all without regard to race or color was an attempt to project legislation that was manifestly unconstitutional, and which this proposed amendment is to make legal. . . .

## Blacks Should Be Allowed Only Certain Rights

In devotion to and love of my country, I will yield to no man on earth. My only hope for liberty is in the full restoration of all the States, with the rights of representation in the Congress of the United States upon no condition but to take the oath laid down in the Constitution. In the legislation by the States they should look to the protection, security, advancement, and improvement, physically and intellectually, of all classes, as

37

well the blacks as the whites. Negroes should have the channels of education opened to them by the States, and by the States they should be protected in life, liberty, and property, and by the States should be allowed all the rights of being witnesses, of suing and being sued, of contracting, and doing every act or thing that a white man is authorized by law to do. But to give to them the right of suffrage, and hold office, and marry whites, in my judgment is dangerous and never ought to be extended to them by any State. However, that is a matter belonging solely to the sovereign will of the States. I have faith in the people, and dark and gloomy as the hour is, I do not despair of free government. I plant myself upon the will of God to work out a bright destiny for the American people. . . .

Who gave the Senate the constitutional power to pass that bill guarantying equal rights to all [the Civil Rights Act of 1866] if it is necessary to amend the organic law in the manner proposed by this joint resolution? This is but another attempt to consolidate the power of the States in the Federal Government. It is another step to an imperial despotism. It is but another attempt to blot out from that flag the eleven stars that represent the States of the South and to consolidate in the Federal Government, by the action of Congress, all the powers claimed by the Czar of Russia or the Emperor of the French. It provides that all persons in the several States shall have equal protection in the right of life, liberty, and property. Now, it is claimed by gentlemen upon the other side of the House that negroes are citizens of the United States. Suppose that in the State of New Jersey negroes are citizens, as they are claimed to be by the other side of the House, and they change their residence to the State of South Carolina, if this amendment be passed Congress can pass under it a law compelling South Carolina to grant to negroes every right accorded to white people there; and as white men there have the right to marry white women, negroes, under this amendment, would be entitled to the same right; and thus miscegenation and mixture of the races could be authorized in any State, as all citizens under this amendment are entitled to the same privileges and immunities, and the same protection in life, liberty, and property. . . .

The organic law says that no person but a natural-born citizen, or a citizen when it was made, shall be eligible to the office of President. This amendment would make all citizens eligible, negroes as well as whites. For if negroes are citizens, they are natural born because they are the descendants of ancestors for several generations back, who were born here as well as themselves. The negroes cannot be citizens in a new State in which they may take up their residence unless they are entitled to the privileges and immunities of the citizens resident in that State. Most of the States make a distinction in the rights of married women. This would authorize Congress to repeal all such distinctions.

## The Amendment Would Mean Racial Intermarriage and School Desegregation

Marriage is a contract as set down in all the books from the Year-books down to the present time. A white citizen of any State may marry a white woman; but if a black citizen goes into the same State he is entitled to the same privileges and immunities that white citizens have, and therefore under this amendment a negro might be allowed to marry a white woman. . . .

Now, sir, the words "privileges and immunities" in the Constitution of the United States have been construed by the courts of the several States to mean privileges and immunities in a limited extent. It was so expressly decided in Massachusetts by Chief Justice [Isaac] Parker, one of the ablest judges who ever sat upon the bench in the United States. Those words, as now contained in the Constitution of the United

States, were used in a qualified sense, and subject to the local control, dominion, and the sovereignty of the States. But this act of Congress proposes to amend the Constitution so as to take away the rights of the States with regard to the life, liberty, and property of the people, so as to enable and empower Congress to pass laws compelling the abrogation of all the statutes of the States which makes a distinction, for instance, between a crime committed by a white man and a crime committed by a black man, or allow white people privileges, immunities, or property not allowed to a black man.

Take the State of Kentucky, for instance. According to her laws, if a negro commits a rape upon a white woman he is punished by death. If a white man commits that offense, the punishment is imprisonment. Now, according to this proposed amendment, the Congress of the United States is to have the right to repeal the law of Kentucky and compel that State to inflict the same punishment upon a white man for rape as upon a black man.

According to the organic law of Indiana a negro is forbidden to come there and hold property. This amendment would abrogate and blot out forever that law, which is valuable in the estimation of the sovereign people of Indiana.

In the State of Pennsylvania there are laws which make a distinction with regard to the schooling of white children and the schooling of black children. It is provided that certain schools shall be designated and set apart for white children, and certain other schools designated and set apart for black children. Under this amendment, Congress would have power to compel the State to provide for white children and black children to attend the same school, upon the principle that all the people in the several States shall have equal protection in all the rights of life, liberty, and property, and all the privileges and immunities of citizens in the several States. . . .

Does this amendment propose to leave the several States foreign to each other as regards the regulation of property and of estates, the laws of marriage and divorce, and the protection of the powers of those who live under their jurisdiction? No, sir; it proposes to take away all those rights of a State, and under this broad principle of equality which during the last five years has been proclaimed throughout the land to empower the Federal Government to exercise an absolute, despotic, uncontrollable power of entering the domain of the States and saying to them, "Your State laws must be repealed wherever they do not give to the colored population of the country the same rights and privileges to which your white citizens are entitled."

# Call for the House of Representatives to Vote on the Fourteenth Amendment

*Thaddeus Stevens*

*The following excerpt is taken from a speech made by Thaddeus Stevens of Pennsylvania in the U.S. House of Representatives on June 13, 1866. In it, Stevens calls for a vote on the Fourteenth Amendment, the draft of which had just been revised by the Senate. Although he was not satisfied with the final version, his objections had nothing to do with its Equal Protection Clause; rather, they concerned provisions of the sections dealing with the readmission of the Southern states to the Union. (Later, he led the attempt to impeach President Andrew Johnson, whom he criticizes in this speech.) Stevens believed that blacks in all states should have the right to vote, but he did not live to see that happen; he died in 1868, a few weeks after the Fourteenth Amendment was ratified and more than a year before the ratification of the Fifteenth Amendment. Twenty thousand people, half of them free blacks, attended his funeral.*

*Thaddeus Stevens, a member of the U.S. House of Representatives from Pennsylvania, was one of the most powerful members of Congress during the Civil War and Reconstruction eras. His chief focus for many years had been the abolition of slavery and the granting of rights to blacks and other minorities. He was the leader of the Radical Republicans, who controlled Congress starting in 1866, and was among the chief backers of the Fourteenth Amendment.*

M r. Speaker, I do not intend to detain the House long. A few words will suffice.

We may, perhaps, congratulate the House and the country on the near approach to completion of a proposition to be

Thaddeus Stevens, U.S. House of Representatives, June 13, 1866. *Congressional Globe*, 39th Congress, pp. 3148–49. http://lcweb2.loc.gov/ammem/amlaw/lwcg.html.

submitted to the people for the admission of an outlawed community into the privileges and advantages of a civilized and free Government.

When I say that we should rejoice at such completion, I do not thereby intend so much to express joy at the superior excellence of the scheme, as that there is to be a scheme—a scheme containing much positive good, as well, I am bound to admit, as the omission of many better things.

In my youth, in my manhood, in my old age, I had fondly dreamed that when any fortunate chance should have broken up for awhile the foundation of our institutions, and released us from obligations the most tyrannical that ever man imposed in the name of freedom, that the intelligent, pure and just men of this Republic, true to their professions and their consciences, would have so remodeled all our institutions as to have freed them from every vestige of human oppression, of inequality of rights, of the recognized degradation of the poor, and the superior caste of the rich. In short, that no distinction would be tolerated in this purified Republic but what arose from merit and conduct. This bright dream has vanished "like the baseless fabric of a vision." [A quotation from Shakespeare's play *The Tempest*.] I find that we shall be obliged to be content with patching up the worst portions of the ancient edifice, and leaving it, in many of its parts, to be swept through by the tempests, the frosts, and the storms of despotism.

## The Amendment Is Not Perfect

Do you inquire why, holding these views and possessing some will of my own, I accept so imperfect a proposition? I answer, because I live among men and not among angels; among men as intelligent, as determined, and as independent as myself, who, not agreeing with me, do not choose to yield their opinions to mine. Mutual concession, therefore, is our only resort, or mutual hostilities.

[Printer's No., 177.

39TH CONGRESS,
1ST SESSION.

# H. R. 543.

## IN THE HOUSE OF REPRESENTATIVES.

APRIL 30, 1866.

Read twice, ordered to be printed, and made a special order for Wednesday, May 9th, after reading the journal, and from day to day until disposed of.

Mr. STEVENS, from the Joint Select Committee on Reconstruction, reported the following bill:

# A BILL

To provide for restoring to the States lately in insurrection their full political rights.

Whereas it is expedient that the States lately in insurrection should, at the earliest day consistent with the future peace and safety of the Union, be restored to full participation in all political rights; and whereas the Congress did, by joint resolution, propose for ratification to the legislatures of the several States, as an amendment to the Constitution of the United States, an article in the following words, to wit:

"ARTICLE —.

"SECTION 1. No State shall make or enforce any law which shall abridge the privileges or immunities of citizens of the United States; nor shall any State deprive any person of life, liberty, or property, without due process of law; nor deny to any person within its jurisdiction the equal protection of the laws.

"SECTION 2. Representatives shall be apportioned among

*A portion of the original House version of the bill that became the Fourteenth Amendment.*

We might well have been justified in making renewed and more strenuous efforts for a better plan could we have had the coöperation of the Executive [the president]. With this cordial assistance the rebel States might have been made model republics, and this nation an empire of universal freedom. But he preferred "restoration" to "reconstruction.". . .

A few words will suffice to explain the changes made by the Senate in the proposition which we sent them.

The first section is altered by defining who are citizens of the United States and of the States. This is an excellent amendment, long needed to settle conflicting decisions between the several States and the United States. It declares this great privilege to belong to every person born naturalized in the United States. . . .

## The Amendment Must Be Adopted Before Opposition Increases

You perceive that while I see much good in the proposition I do not pretend to be satisfied with it. And yet I am anxious for its speedy adoption, for I dread delay. The danger is that before any constitutional guards shall have been adopted Congress will be flooded by rebels and rebel sympathizers. Whoever has mingled much in deliberative bodies must have observed the mental as well as physical nervousness of many members, impelling them too often to injudicious action. Whoever has watched the feelings of this House during the tedious months of this session, listened to the impatient whispering of some and the open declarations of others; especially when able and sincere men propose to gratify personal predilections by breaking the ranks of the Union forces and presenting to the enemy a ragged front of stragglers, must be anxious to hasten the result and prevent the demoralization of our friends. Hence, I say, let us no longer delay; take what we can get now, and hope for better things in further legislation; in enabling acts or other provisions.

# Speech in the House of Representatives Praising the Fourteenth Amendment

*Jehu Baker*

*The following selection is a portion of a speech made by Jehu Baker in the U.S. House of Representatives on July 9, 1866, about the importance of the Fourteenth Amendment to the nation. It was the custom at that time for very long, philosophical speeches to be made in Congress. In this one, Baker expresses ideas not only about the amendment's provisions but also about the nature of human progress, some of which are well worth pondering today. When Baker speaks of "these late bloody years," he is referring to the Civil War, which had just ended; but his belief that progress does occur, however slow it may seem, could apply to any era in which people are discouraged by evils that cannot be quickly eliminated. Baker views the Fourteenth Amendment as a strong sign of progress, and at the end of his speech he expresses a strong conviction that it will be ratified.*

*Jehu Baker, a lawyer, represented the state of Illinois in Congress from 1866 to 1869. He later served two more terms, from 1887 to 1889 and from 1897 to 1899.*

After long, earnest, and laborious consideration, this Congress, by very great majorities in both Houses, has agreed upon a fundamental basis for the pacification and future security of the Republic. As it was plainly necessary that the nation, and not its late enemies, should take into its own hands the keeping of its own securities, it clearly resulted that the great terms of the arrangement should go into the Constitu-

Jehu Baker, U.S. House of Representatives, July 9, 1866. *Appendix to the Congressional Globe*, 39th Congress, pp. 255–58. http://lcweb2.loc.gov/ammem/amlaw/lwcg.html.

tion of the country. Accordingly, the plan presented consists of a proposed amendment of the Constitution, made up of five sections.

This amendment I regard as one of immense value. Though it may not make our Constitution ideally perfect, or embrace all that many desired, yet it is full of strong, practical, and most valuable provisions; valuable for the safety of the Republic, and valuable for the security and future growth of liberty. On the whole, I regard it as a very fair expression of the average sense and average culture of the great popular mind of the country.

And I will say here, that as I apprehend it, the growth of institutions and liberties in any country is and must be but the forward movement of this average sense and culture. In the development of its civilization, the whole of a national society, and especially of a democratic society, must be looked at as one individual organism, impelled by one aggregate life force; from which it results that the social and institutional progress of the community will conform itself, not to the highest thought and aspiration in the State, nor yet to the lowest, but, as I have said, to the general average of the whole mass.

## Progress Occurs Step by Step

This being one of the laws, higher than any of human enactment, which governs the progress of nations and the growth of civilization, every truly wise thinker, freighted though his mind may be with darling conceptions which he longs to see completely realized, will accept it as a providential arrangement, content himself with adding one additional stone to the edifice of ages, and thus contrive to keep his soul in peace. . . .

We may gather some cheer from the reflection, that though civilization in all lands is still blundering in its alphabet, yet the realized fact of to-day is higher than the most famous ideal embodiments of the past; for we have here in our own country an actual subsisting polity incomparably superior as a whole to anything we read of in the *Republic* of Plato, the *New Atlantis* of Bacon, the *Oceana* of Harrington, or the *Utopia* of More [works that described ideal societies]. In view of this great law, which slowly evolves, step by step, the progress of human society, as of universal physical nature, we may learn to chasten our impatience without abating our zeal, and to accept thankfully for the time the best measure of good we are able to attain. If liberty will not grow in advance of culture, if in politics as in hydraulics the stream will not flow above the fountain head, it is no fault of ours, nor of God's either. Deep down at the bottom of the being of things, further down than finite intelligence may ever be able to penetrate, I make no question there is a complete moral justification of that wonderful arrangement, by which the individual, the social, the moral, the political, and religious life of mankind must pass by gradual advances, and through suffering, labor, and patient endurance, into the higher goods of liberty and virtue. If it seem that the wine press of affliction we have trod during these late bloody years should yield more perfect immediate results, we may doubt whether our national culture has been equal to our national affliction, and we may know that the blood of the martyrs of humanity, like all other seed, does not instantly spring from the ground and flower forth into the full fruition of human uses. Now, and in the future, the utmost return will be made for the late prodigious heroism and suffering of the nation.

Most encouraging is that profound change for the better which has already taken place in our public life and public thought. . . .

## The Amendment's First Section Will Be "Jewel of Beauty"

Content with the possibilities of the present, nothing doubting the better realizations of the future, let us briefly analyze this

## HARPER'S WEEKLY.
### JOURNAL OF CIVILIZATION

VOL. IX.—No. 425.]     NEW YORK, SATURDAY, FEBRUARY 18, 1865.     [SINGLE COPIES TEN CENTS.
[$4.00 PER YEAR IN ADVANCE.

Entered according to Act of Congress, in the Year 1865, by Harper & Brothers, in the Clerk's Office of the District Court for the Southern District of New York.

SCENE IN THE HOUSE ON THE PASSAGE OF THE PROPOSITION TO AMEND THE CONSTITUTION, JANUARY 31, 1865.

*House of Representatives, drawing.* Harper's Weekly, *February 18, 1865.*

Reconstruction Amendment which we have tendered to the States as a practical basis for the restored political order of the Union.

Indeed, comment upon the several sections which compose this amendment may well be brief; for there are some propositions, the justice and propriety of which are so obvious in their simple statement, that they cannot be much helped by any amount of argument or illustration.

The first section of the amendment is as follows:

> "Sec. 1. All persons born or naturalized in the United States, and subject to the jurisdiction thereof, are citizens of the United States and of the State wherein they reside. No State shall make or enforce any law which shall abridge the privileges or immunities of citizens of the United States; nor shall any State deprive any person of life, liberty, or property, without due process of law, nor deny to any person within its jurisdiction the equal protection of the laws."

This section I regard as more valuable for clearing away bad interpretations and bad uses of the Constitution as it is than for any positive grant of new power which it contains. How admirable, how plainly just, are the several provisions of it!

> "All persons born or naturalized in the United States, and subject to the jurisdiction thereof, are citizens of the United States and of the State wherein they reside."

Who can object to this? Persons born or naturalized in the United States, and subject to its jurisdiction, subject to taxation, to military service, to all the burdens of society, both State and national, *ought*, upon every principle of manly justice, to receive in turn from society that protection which is involved in the *status* of citizenship. To compel a man to submit to your jurisdiction in all things, to pay your taxes, and fight your battles, and then withhold from him this reasonable measure of reciprocal protection is, to say the least, and to call it by no harder name, a political villainy which every citizen of a democratic country ought to be ashamed of. Again:

> "No State shall make or enforce any law which shall abridge the privileges or immunities of citizens of the United States."

What business is it of any State to do the things here forbidden? To rob the American citizen of rights thrown around him by the supreme law of the land? When we remember to what an extent this has been done in the past, we can appreciate the need of putting a stop to it in the future. Again:

"Nor shall any State deprive any person of life, liberty, or property without due process of law, nor deny to any person within its jurisdiction the equal protection of the laws."

How clearly right and necessary to liberty is this! The Constitution already declares generally that no person shall "be deprived of life, liberty, or property without due process of law." This declares particularly that no *State* shall do it—a wholesome and needed check upon the great abuse of liberty which several of the States have practiced, and which they manifest too much purpose to continue. The final clause of the section, providing that no State shall deny to any person within its jurisdiction the equal protection of the laws, is so obviously right, that one would imagine nobody could be found so hard-hearted and cruel as not to recognize its simple justice. Is it not a disgrace to a free country that the poor and the weak members of society should be denied equal justice and equal protection at the hands of the law? Who can look straight at the fact till he realizes its full meaning and its full meanness without dropping his eyes and hanging his head in shame? This whole section is sound in all its parts and in every particular. It appeals irresistibly to the democratic instinct of the people, and it will be a jewel of beauty when placed in the Constitution of the country. . . .

## The Amendment Will Be Ratified

Sir, as there is a time for all things, so there are things which are appropriate to each period of time. Late the martial drumbeat was heard through all our borders, and the deep-throated cannon was dragged to fields of carnage and death. War, furious, relentless, consuming war, was then the duty of the hour—made its duty in order that the Republic might not be blotted from the map of nations. After the most tremendous conflict of the age if not of history, the flag of treason and slavery went down before the banner of the Republic. The smoke has cleared away from the battle-field; the moldering dead, sown thick as the leaves of the forest, sleep quietly in the long battle-trenches where they fell; the green grass of summer is made greener by the blood that enriched the soil. O, God! how revolting is the thought, that the coming harvest of such a sowing should be prematurely blighted by the same hand that cast the seed! that the people which gave its children to the slaughter, and made itself immortal by its heroic endurance and its deeds of valor, should now prove itself incompetent to make secure and fruitful the peace it has conquered at so great a cost! It is impossible! It is impossible! There is too much intelligence, and patriotism, and nobleness of mind and heart in this great people, to allow such an ignoble and detestable fact to have a place in their history! The imperative public duty that now lies next our hand will be performed! The amendment proposed by this Congress as a basis of safe and permanent pacification—so just to the Nation, so just to the South, and so just in itself—will be sustained and placed in the Constitution of the Republic. Then—the country made secure from the perils which still threaten it—every star restored to more than its former luster in the azure field of the national escutcheon—we shall move upon the future with firm and assured footstep, meeting, as I trust in God successfully, the ever new and momentous duties which that future shall bring.

# New York Times Editorial Following Ratification of the Fourteenth Amendment

*New York Times*

*This editorial appeared in the* New York Times *shortly after ratification of the Fourteenth Amendment. It describes the opposition to the amendment and expresses regret that it was not accepted sooner by the Southern states—which, in the opinion of the author, would have avoided the imposition of military governments there and eliminated "all sectional jealousies." This, of course, was a controversial opinion, with which Southerners would not have agreed. The editorial concludes by warning that the Democrats "now threaten to abrogate" (ignore) the amendment, which did happen in many cases. The Democratic Party at that time favored leniency toward the defeated South and was for many years dominant there. It succeeded in depriving Southern blacks of many of the rights guaranteed to them by the Fourteenth and Fifteenth amendments. However, Democrats in the North opposed the amendment not because of the rights it gave to blacks but because they believed it gave too much power to the federal government, a concern the editorial fails to mention.*

The Fourteenth Amendment to the Constitution of the United States has been ratified and is now a part of the organic law [the fundamental laws of the United States, including the Declaration of Independence, the Articles of Confederation, and the Constitution]—to which fact we invite the attention of Democrats, who profess so obsequious an observance of "the Constitution and the laws." On the 15th [of July, 1868] the President transmitted to Congress a letter from Secretary [of State William H.] SEWARD, announcing the ratifica-

*New York Times*, Editorial, July 17, 1868.

---

### Ratification of the Fourteenth Amendment

| | | |
|---|---|---|
| Alabama | July 13, 1868 | |
| Arkansas | April 6, 1868 | |
| California | May 6, 1959 | |
| Connecticut | June 25, 1866 | |
| Delaware | February 12, 1901 | (After rejecting on February 7, 1867) |
| Florida | June 9, 1868 | |
| Georgia | July 21, 1868 | (After rejecting on November 9, 1866) |
| Illinois | January 15, 1867 | |
| Indiana | January 23, 1867 | |
| Iowa | March 16, 1868 | |
| Kansas | January 11, 1867 | |
| Kentucky | March 18, 1976 | (After rejecting on January 8, 1867) |
| Louisiana | July 9, 1868 | (After rejecting on February 6, 1867) |
| Maine | January 19, 1867 | |
| Maryland | April 4, 1959 | (After rejecting on March 23, 1867) |
| Massachusetts | March 20, 1867 | |
| Michigan | January 16, 1867 | |
| Minnesota | January 16, 1867 | |
| Mississippi | January 17, 1870 | |
| Missouri | January 25, 1867 | |

**continued**

---

tion of this amendment by the Legislatures of twenty-three Northern States, including Tennessee; and also by Arkansas, Florida and North Carolina. To these twenty-six States must be added Louisiana, South Carolina and Alabama. Here then are twenty-nine States, so that even if we except Ohio and New-Jersey, whose Legislatures have attempted to undo their work, we have the requisite three-fourths of the States, which, according to the Constitution, makes the amendment a part of our Constitution.

## The Opposition to the Amendment

This Amendment was supported by every Republican member of both Houses in the Thirty-ninth Congress, and was opposed by every Democratic member. In the twenty-three State

| Ratification of the Fourteenth Amendment [CONTINUED] | | |
| --- | --- | --- |
| Tennessee | July 19, 1866 | |
| Texas | February 18, 1870 | (After rejecting on October 27, 1866) |
| Vermont | October 30, 1866 | |
| Virginia | October 8, 1869 | (After rejecting on January 9, 1867) |
| West Virginia | January 16,1867 | |
| Wisconsin | February 7, 1867 | |

TAKEN FROM: Compiled by editor.

Legislatures at the North the same party-line was drawn. The Democratic Legislatures of Delaware, Maryland and Kentucky rejected the Amendment, and this year, the Democrats having a majority in the Ohio and New-Jersey Legislatures, have repealed the act of ratification; notwithstanding the majorities in these States in its favor in 1866. It was opposed by President [Andrew] JOHNSON, who sent a telegram to Gov. [Lewis] PARSONS, advising the Legislature of Alabama against its ratification. The Amendment was rejected by every Southern State except Tennessee, which latter State by its adoption was restored to the Union. If it had been accepted by the South as the basis of restoration, reconstruction would have been an accomplished fact two years ago; no military governments would have been imposed upon the South, and all sectional jealousies would have been obliterated.

And why should it not have been accepted? It simply proclaimed that all citizens born or naturalized in the United States were citizens of the United States and of the State in which they resided; it prohibited laws abridging the privileges or immunities of citizens, or denying to any citizen the equal protection of the laws; it did not impose negro suffrage, but in case the franchise should not be given to negroes, it reduced representation accordingly; it temporarily disabled from holding office all those who, after taking an oath, "as a member of Congress, or as an officer of the United States, or as a member of any State Legislature, or as an executive or judicial officer of any State," had afterward engaged in rebellion, leaving this disability to be removed by Congress so soon as expediency required; it declared the validity of our public debt, and it repudiated all obligations incurred by rebellion, and all claims for compensation on account of emancipation.

All these conditions of restoration were explicitly demanded by the people, and were sustained by their votes in the elections of 1866. They were rejected only by the Democratic Party and its Southern allies.

But, in spite of opposition, the amendment has triumphed. The Fortieth Congress made its adoption the principal condition of restoration. If Congress appealed to the negro vote to accomplish this, it was driven to that extremity by the Democrats who opposed it, in the first instance, and who now threaten its abrogation.

# Speech in the House of Representatives Opposing Enforcement of the Fourteenth Amendment

*William S. Holman*

*In 1871 a bill—later known as the Enforcement Act, the Ku Klux Klan Act, or the Civil Rights Act of 1871—was being debated in Congress. It was intended to enforce the provisions of the Fourteenth Amendment's first section, which were being violated in the South by the terrorist activities of the Ku Klux Klan, a white supremacist organization. The bill provided that any person who conspired to deprive another person of his or her constitutional rights could be held criminally liable in federal court, even if the action was not illegal by state law, and it gave the president the power to use the army and navy to quell domestic disturbances. It also provided, among other things, that anyone who deprived someone of his or her rights, or caused them to be deprived, could be sued in state or federal court. (The bill was passed, though portions of it were later ruled unconstitutional by the U.S. Supreme Court; its authorization of civil rights suits remains in effect today.) The following selection is part of a speech made in opposition to this bill by Congressman William S. Holman in the U.S. House of Representatives on April 4, 1871. Holman argues that the law would give the federal government power belonging to the states and that it is unnecessary because if state laws violate the Fourteenth Amendment, the Supreme Court will declare them void.*

*William S. Holman, a lawyer and judge, represented Indiana in Congress for many terms, not all of them consecutive. He was*

William S. Holman, U.S. House of Representatives, April 4, 1871. *Appendix to the Congressional Globe*, 42nd Congress, pp. 257–259. http://lcweb2.loc.gov/ammem/amlaw/lwcg.html.

*a Democrat, which at the time meant that he supported the right of states, including the Southern states, to make their own laws.*

I am not willing that it shall be stated that members on this side of the House [the Democrats] oppose this bill because they are indifferent to the disorder and violence alleged to exist in the South, without an unequivocal denial. The attempt to make such an impression on the country is disingenuous and unjustifiable. The truth is, that with a full knowledge of all the facts which are now known, and overwhelming majority of the House, a majority of the Republican members, decided time and again, prior to the coming in of the President's message, that legislation on this subject was inexpedient until more reliable information should be obtained through a committee of the House. . . .

But we desire to know the actual condition of affairs in the South. We have uniformly favored the fullest investigation. Southern Representatives have courted such investigations, and there is not a member on this side of the House who would oppose any measure necessary to uphold the constitutional powers of the Federal Government in every State of the Union.

That Congress possesses the power to enforce the laws of the United States in every State of the Union no one can deny; that Congress possesses the power to legislate on and regulate the local and domestic affairs of the States of this Union no one can maintain. For myself, sir, before the war and during the war and since the war I have maintained on this floor the right and duty of Congress to enforce the laws of the United States in every State. I am, sir, as anxious to see the just powers of the Federal Government maintained as the just powers of the State governments. In my judgment, the free institutions of this country depend on the equal maintenance of both; the supremacy of the one is the road to despotism, of the other to intestine war and anarchy.

## The Bill Gives the Federal Government Power That Belongs to the States

The bill before us opens new issues. We enter upon an unexplored field. While it is admitted by the advocates of this bill that under the Constitution, prior to the fourteenth amendment, no such powers as are embraced in this bill could be exercised by Congress, it is claimed that that amendment does confer upon Congress these extraordinary powers. By the first and second sections of this bill a new and extended jurisdiction, civil and criminal, is conferred upon the Federal courts, and that, too, in fact, as to matters local to the State and involved in its domestic government; and in the same spirit by the third and fourth sections Congress proposes to take charge of those duties which essentially belong to States, which are indeed the principal duties of States, of vindicating the rights of life, liberty, and property.

It is for these purposes that State governments are formed. And by these two sections of this bill, under this power to regulate the domestic affairs of States, very naturally the executive power is increased to an extent that could not have been dreamed of by the men who formed this Government. . . .

But, sir [the Speaker of the House], all history and every lesson we have learned from our fathers admonish us not to increase the executive power, and to maintain the clear line of demarkation between the national powers of government and the proper local self-government of the States.

It is claimed that the first and last sections of the fourteenth amendment of the Constitution authorize the passage of this bill. Indeed, the title of the bill assumes this: "A bill to enforce the provisions of the fourteenth amendment to the Constitution of the United States, and for other purposes."

The first section of the fourteenth amendment is as follows:

"SEC. 1. All persons born or naturalized in the United States, and subject to the jurisdiction thereof, are citizens of the United States and of the State wherein they reside. No State shall make or enforce any law which shall abridge the privileges or immunities of citizens of the United States; nor shall any State deprive any person of life, liberty, or property without due process of law, nor deny to any person within its jurisdiction the equal protection of the laws."

And the last section is as follows:

"SEC. 5. The Congress shall have power to enforce by appropriate legislation the provisions of this articles."

It does not seem that this last section of the fourteenth amendment has any possible reference to the first section, but it has manifestly reference only to the second and third sections of the fourteenth amendment, both of which clearly require the action of Congress; but the first confers on Congress no powers of legislation. The Constitution of the United States and laws made under it operate not upon States, but upon the whole people, and herein lies the fact that the Constitution does not form a league of States but forms a nation.

The gentleman from Ohio [Mr. Samuel Shellabarger] claims that the first clause of this section, "All persons born or naturalized in the United States, and subject to the jurisdiction thereof, are citizens of the United States and of the State wherein they reside;" confers this power on Congress; that this clause alone creates citizens of the United States. What proposition can be more absurd?. . .

The other clauses of this first section are clearly limitations on States:

"No State shall make or enforce any law which shall abridge the privileges or immunities of citizens of the United States,"—

"No State shall make or enforce any law which shall abridge." Here is simply a limitation on the powers of the States—

*Despite Holman's opposition to the Civil Rights Act of 1871, the bill was passed, giving African Americans the right to vote.*

"nor shall any States deprive any person of life, liberty, or property without due process of law."

"No State shall deprive." Is not this a positive limitation and nothing more? Is it a grant of any power to Congress? "Nor deny to any person within its jurisdiction the equal protection of the laws."

If I understand gentlemen correctly, it is mainly on this last clause they predicate the power of Congress to pass this bill, and yet it seems impossible that this limitation upon the powers of the States should be tortured into an affirmative power in Congress to legislate on that subject. Where power is conferred on Congress by the Constitution it is done in express terms, or as a necessary incident to a power of legislation expressly conferred; but here there is no power conferred, but simply a denial of power. "Nor" shall any State "deny to any person within its jurisdiction the equal protection of the laws." Plain, simple language which admits of no interpretation, for there is no ambiguity.

# If States Laws Violate the Fourteenth Amendment, the Supreme Court Will Declare Them Void

A State, as used in the Constitution, always means the organized political body. No State shall "deny." Can Congress assume that this constitutional injunction will be violated by a State? A State can only act through her legislative department, and if any State does violate either one of these provisions of this first section of the fourteenth amendment, it must be done by some affirmative act of law, and then, sir, what is the remedy? Can there be any doubt of the remedy? The Federal courts—the Supreme Court of the United States, to which is confided the duty of vindicating the Constitution from infraction, either by the acts of Congress or the acts of any State, declares the statute null and void. Yes, sir, void; and here the Constitution provides for its own vindication. The fifth amendment of the Constitution declares that no person shall "be deprived of life, liberty, or property without due process of law." This is a limitation on Congress, and now this fourteenth amendment imposes the same limitation on the power of the States.

Suppose that either Congress or any State should enact a law in violation of this provision; does any one doubt the completeness of the remedy? No, sir. The Supreme Court will declare the law void. Let either Congress or a State violate the Constitution, and that august tribunal, one of the three great departments of your Government, declares the law void. It is not by the Army and Navy and the suspension of the great writ of right in a time of peace that either States or Congress are restrained from violating constitutional limitations. No, sir; it is by the peaceful power of an impartial tribunal of justice from which neither Congress nor the States can appeal. Here, sir, the Constitution has lodged the power to vindicate its sacred guarantees of life, liberty, and property alike against the encroachments of Congress and of States.

It is clear, sir, that if Congress can under this fourteenth amendment, interfere at all in the local affairs of the States, if these denials of power to the States are to be construed as conferring legislative power on Congress, there is then no limitation on the powers of Congress in respect to the domestic affairs of States; from being a Government of the limited powers delegated by the Constitution, its powers become absolute and without limit. If this section of the fourteenth amendment does confer any power on Congress, can any man say where the limit of that power is? I will not believe that the people intended anything like this in the adoption of the fourteenth amendment. I know they did not. Even in the midst of the then ebbing tumults of terrible war through which we had passed public attention would have been arrested at the idea of conferring such power upon the Federal Government. The people who so bravely supported the Federal power in the struggle for the Union never intended that the domestic governments of the States should be stricken down. They know, sir, that their liberties rest only secure in the just balance of political power.

# Speech in the Senate Favoring Enforcement of the Fourteenth Amendment

*Henry Wilson*

*The following selection is a portion of a speech made by Henry Wilson in the U.S. Senate on April 13, 1871, in support of the bill that would be known variously as the Enforcement Act, the Ku Klux Klan Act, or the Civil Rights Act of 1871. It is a political speech, and like all such speeches, then and now, it uses strong language to criticize one party and glorify the other. However, it was true that the Democrats of the post–Civil War period opposed enforcement of the Fourteenth Amendment by the federal government—which they believed would take too much power away from the states—and that those in the South blamed the Republicans, who controlled Congress, for Reconstruction policies that they perceived as oppressive. The Republican Party, then quite a new party, had risen to power on a platform of abolishing slavery, an accomplishment in which it naturally took pride. In his speech Senator Wilson is expressing his admiration for the bill rather than seeking votes for it; because there were at the time fifty-seven Republicans in the Senate and only seventeen Democrats, its passage was a foregone conclusion.*

*Henry Wilson, originally a shoemaker, was a U.S. senator from Massachusetts from 1855 to 1873. He was chairman of the Senate Committee on Military Affairs throughout the Civil War and served as vice president of the United States from 1873 until his death in 1875.*

Sir, the inhuman legislation, the oppressive acts, the appalling crimes, the deeds of inhumanity, and the earnest appeals of the freedmen for protection, penetrated the ear and

Henry Wilson, U.S. Senate, April 13, 1871. *Appendix to the Congressional Globe*, 42nd Congress, pp. 255–257. http://lcweb2.loc.gov/ammem/amlaw/lwcg.html.

touched the heart of the nation. Congress passed an act to secure to the freedmen civil rights. A joint special committee of fifteen was raised in December, 1865. This committee was composed of gentlemen of talent and experience, of individual honor and personal character. Its report, by its eminent chairman, William Pitt Fessenden, referred to the conciliatory measures of the Government, and declared that—

"The bitterness and defiance exhibited toward the United States, under such circumstances, is without a parallel in the history of the world. In return for our leniency we receive only an insulting denial of our authority. In return for our kind desire for the resumption of fraternal relations we receive only an insolent assumption of rights and privileges long since forfeited. The crime we have punished is paraded as a virtue, and the principles of republican government, which we have vindicated at so terrible a cost, are denounced as unjust and oppressive."

This report demonstrated with great clearness and force the duty of the nation to secure liberty, life, person, and property, and "to place our republican institutions on a more stable foundation." It proposed to accomplish these purposes by an amendment to the Constitution, known as the fourteenth amendment. Through the year 1866 the civil rights act was practically a dead letter, and the proposed amendment to the Constitution was contemptuously rejected by the States lately in rebellion.

## The Reconstruction Acts

At the next session of Congress, under the lead of Thaddeus Stevens, the joint committee of fifteen on reconstruction was empowered to act; and this committee reported a measure for the more effectual government of the rebel States, which became a law on the 2d of March, 1867. The President's policy had placed ten of the eleven rebel States completely under the control of those who had carried them into rebellion. Loyal

*Henry Wilson was United States Senator for Massachusetts from 1854 to 1873.* The Library of Congress.

men were utterly powerless and without protection. The freedmen were free only in name. This great measure struck down the usurped power of a privileged class of disloyal men, gave protection to the loyal and the ballot to the freedmen. It was followed by the act of the 23d of March, providing a plan of reconstruction. These two great measures of reconstruction sought to rescue the South from the domination of privilege and caste, to give the government to the people, and enable those who were loyal to their country to reconstruct government upon the enduring basis of equal rights and equal privileges. They sought to give peace, law, order, education, and development to the section of the country blighted by slavery, scarred by civil war, and demoralized by lawlessness and violence.

Such, Mr. President [the president of the Senate, i.e., the U.S. vice president], were those grand measures of reconstruction pronounced by the Democratic national convention of 1868 to be "unconstitutional, revolutionary, and void," declared by the honorable Senator from Missouri [Mr. Francis Preston BLAIR Jr.] to be usurpations to be trampled "into dust," and for the passage of which Congress has been stigmatized by him in this debate as "the original Ku Klax" [Ku Klux Klan]. . . .

For several months the prejudices and hatreds against the colored race, intensified by political animosities, manifested themselves in bloody deeds. In Louisiana, in a few weeks preceding the [presidential] election nearly a thousand were killed outright, and nearly an equal number wounded and maltreated. These bloody acts decided the result of the election, contrary to the well-ascertained will of the people. In Georgia the Camilla massacre and the scourgings and murders in other portions of that State, kept tens of thousands of men from exercising the right of suffrage, guarantied to them by the law of the country and the new constitution of that State. Outrages were perpetrated upon the freedmen in other southern States, but they were not potent enough to affect political results.

## Outrages Committed by the Ku Klux Klan

After the election of General [Ulysses S.] Grant, and the indorsement by the people of the policy of reconstruction, these outrages were largely diminished. In some sections of the South comparative order and quiet have prevailed under the present Administration. The vigorous measures adopted in Arkansas, and now enforced in Texas, have contributed largely to this result. But in some sections there has continued to be much disorder, and during the last few months terrible outrages have been committed, especially by these secret, armed bands of assassins. There is no disguising the fact that the outrages of the last few months have a political significance.

The Ku Klux Klans, be their numbers more or less, are inspired not only by hatred of the negro, but by implacable resentment toward those who have emancipated him and given him civil and political rights. The evidences are conclusive that these organizations are guided by political desires and purposes. They desire to secure to the Democratic party the control of the South and the triumph of the Democratic party in the nation. Their purpose is to effect those results by intimidation, and the results already accomplished by mobbings and burnings, scourgings and murderings, inspire their hopes and tire their zeal.

The victims of these outrages, who have appealed in vain for protection to the judicial tribunals of their States, now appeal to Congress for "the equal protection of the laws." In response to these appeals, it is proposed to enact this bill to enforce the fourteenth amendment to the Constitution. In both Houses the outrages perpetrated by Ku Klux Klans and others are denied or extenuated, and we, who are seeking by national legislation to protect life and liberty, person and property, are denounced in unmeasured terms as violators of the Constitution of our country. So it has ever been. The series of acts by which the slave-masters' rebellion was conquered, four and a half million slaves emancipated, given civil rights and political privileges, were denounced as violations of the Constitution, and we, who have consummated these immortal measures of patriotism and liberty, have been perpetually denounced as the enemies of liberty and of the Constitution, especially by those who raised their hands against their country and sought on bloody fields the overthrow of the Constitution and the death of the Republic.

## Opposition by the Democrats to the Enforcement Act

But their denunciations are passed by us unheeded, and have met no response in the bosoms of our loyal countrymen. We have moved right straight forward and onward in the great work assigned us by the needs of the country and the providence of God. In spite of the fiercest denunciations we have accomplished the grand work assigned us and received the applauding voices of our countrymen and the approval of the civilized world. In the present exigencies of the country I trust that we, unawed by denunciations, will go to the extreme verge of constitutional power to suppress these lawless combinations and protect our countrymen of the South in their lives, their persons, and their property, and in the full exercise of their constitutional rights as citizens of the United States.

Democratic Senators and Representatives find no authority in the Constitution for the enactment of this measure to enforce the fourteenth amendment. . . .

Sir, I see, or I think I see, ample powers in the fourteenth amendment upon which to base the legislation proposed by the pending bill. I concur entirely in the construction put upon that provision of the fourteenth amendment by Mr. [John] Bingham, of Ohio, by whom it was drawn. When gentlemen of eminent ability, of legal acquisitions, and of large experience differ, as they have during the great contests through which the nation has passed, in construing the provisions of the Constitution, I accept those constructions that contribute to the preservation of the country and the conservation of liberty. I reverence the Constitution, but man is more than constitutions. I honor the laws when in harmony with the higher laws of God, but I reverence and honor humanity more. Constitutions and laws were made for man, and should be so framed and so interpreted as to guard and protect the rights which the Creator has bestowed. . . .

When history shall trace on its immortal pages the record of the acts of the Democratic party in support of the wickedest system of bondage the sun ever shone upon, coming generations as they read that story will wonder how men who did such deeds for a relentless despotism were ever impudent enough to arraign any portion of their countrymen for want of fidelity to liberty.

## Achievements by the Republicans Toward Equality for Blacks

Let us contrast, Mr. President, with this inglorious Democratic record the bright record of the Republican party. It came into power ten years ago under the lead of Abraham Lincoln. It found an armed slaveholders' rebellion and a dismembered Union. History must record the glorious fact, for the study and admiration of after-times, that the Republican party was inspired by patriotism and liberty; that it crushed rebellion by the hand of war, and gave freedom to millions of countrymen in bondage. Yes, sir, history must record that the Republicans, denounced in this Chamber as "unjust oppressors," made free slaves used by rebels for military purposes; forbade officers of the Army to return fugitives seeking the protection of the national flag; abolished slavery in the District of Columbia and annulled its inhuman slave code; prohibited slavery in the national Territories; repealed the fugitive slave act; gave freedom to bondmen captured by the armies; recognized the independence of Hayti and Liberia; enrolled black men to fight the battles of their country, and freed their wives and children; sustained President Lincoln's proclamation of emancipation; created the Freedmen's Bureau for the protection and education of emancipated bondmen; extended suffrage to colored men in the District of Columbia and in the Territories; enacted the civil rights bill, securing to black men the full and equal benefit of all laws for the protection of life and property, and the reconstruction measures, securing suffrage to three quarters of a million black men; adopted the thirteenth constitutional amendment forever abolishing slavery throughout the land, the fourteenth amendment providing that no person shall be denied the equal protection of the laws, the fifteenth amendment guarantying suffrage to the colored race; passed the great act to enforce the fifteenth amendment, and several other acts, each and all tending to secure personal liberty and to guard the rights and privileges of a race which had borne centuries of oppression. . .

I trust, Mr. President, that this Congress will add the bill now pending to the long series of enactments of the last five Congresses for the freedom of all, for justice to all, and for the protection of all.

# Equal Protection for
# Racial Minorities

# The Fourteenth Amendment Prohibits Laws That Are Discriminatory in Effect

*Stanley Matthews*

*In the case of* Yick Wo v. Hopkins, *the Supreme Court considered a San Francisco city law that prohibited operating laundries in wooden buildings without permission from the board of supervisors, although it was legal to operate them in brick or stone buildings. Though in theory this law applied to everyone, in practice it applied only to Chinese laundries because their owners could not afford brick or stone buildings—it was clearly designed to give a monopoly to the wealthy white businessmen who could. Of the 320 laundries operating in the city, 310 were built of wood, and most of those were owned by Chinese citizens; only the few owners who were not Chinese were given permission to go on operating them. Yick Wo, who had run a laundry business in the same wooden building for twenty-two years, was unwilling to stop and was jailed for refusing to pay the fine. When his case reached the Supreme Court, the justices ruled unanimously that although the San Francisco ordinance was fair on its face, the way in which it was administered deprived the Chinese of the equal protection of the laws guaranteed by the Constitution's Fourteenth Amendment. This was the first case in which the Equal Protection Clause, which was originally designed to protect the rights of blacks, was applied to another minority group.*

*Stanley Matthews was a justice of the U.S. Supreme Court from 1881 until his death in 1889. He had previously been a colonel in the Union army during the Civil War and, later, a U.S. senator. He is best known for his opinion in* Yick Wo v. Hopkins, *which was far in advance of its time and remains influential today.*

Stanley Matthews, unanimous opinion, *Yick Wo v. Hopkins*, U.S. Supreme Court, May 10, 1886.

The ordinance drawn in question in the present case . . . does not prescribe a rule and conditions, for the regulation of the use of property for laundry purposes, to which all similarly situated may conform. It allows, without restriction, the use for such purposes of buildings of brick or stone; but, as to wooden buildings, constituting nearly all those in previous use, it divides the owners or occupiers into two classes, not having respect to their personal character and qualifications for the business, nor the situation and nature and adaptation of the buildings themselves, but merely by an arbitrary line, on one side of which are those who are permitted to pursue their industry by the mere will and consent of the supervisors, and on the other those from whom that consent is withheld, at their mere will and pleasure. . . .

## The Fourteenth Amendment Is Not Confined to U.S. Citizens

The rights of the petitioners, as affected by the proceedings of which they complain, are not less because they are aliens and subjects of the emperor of China. By the third article of the treaty between this government and that of China, concluded November 17, 1880, it is stipulated: 'If Chinese laborers, or Chinese of any other class, now either permanently or temporarily residing in the territory of the United States, meet with ill treatment at the hands of any other persons, the government of the United States will exert all its powers to devise measures for their protection, and to secure to them the same rights, privileges, immunities, and exemptions as may be enjoyed by the citizens or subjects of the most favored nation, and to which they are entitled by treaty.' The fourteenth amendment to the constitution is not confined to the protection of citizens. It says: 'Nor shall any state deprive any person of life, liberty, or property without due process of law; nor deny to any person within its jurisdiction the equal protection of the laws.' These provisions are universal in their application, to all persons within the territorial jurisdiction, without regard to any differences of race, of color, or of nationality; and the equal protection of the laws is a pledge of the protection of equal laws. It is accordingly enacted by section 1977 of the Revised Statutes that 'all persons within the jurisdiction of the United States shall have the same right, in every state and territory, to make and enforce contracts, to sue, be parties, give evidence, and to the full and equal benefit of all laws and proceedings for the security of persons and property as is enjoyed by white citizens, and shall be subject to like punishment, pains, penalties, taxes, licenses, and exactions of every kind, and to no other.' The questions we have to consider and decide in these cases, therefore, are to be treated as involving the rights of every citizen of the United States equally with those of the strangers and aliens who now invoke the jurisdiction of the court.

It is contended on the part of the petitioners that the ordinances for violations of which they are severally sentenced to imprisonment are void on their face, as being within the prohibitions of the fourteenth amendment, and, in the alternative, if not so, that they are void by reason of their administration, operating unequally, so as to punish in the present petitioners what is permitted to others as lawful, without any distinction of circumstances—an unjust and illegal discrimination, it is claimed, which, though not made expressly by the ordinances, is made possible by them.

When we consider the nature and the theory of our institutions of government, the principles upon which they are supposed to rest, and review the history of their development, we are constrained to conclude that they do not mean to leave room for the play and action of purely personal and arbitrary power. . . . The fundamental rights to life, liberty, and the pursuit of happiness, considered as individual possessions, are secured by those maxims of constitutional law which are the monuments showing the victorious progress of the race in se-

*Justice Stanley Matthews served on the United States Supreme Court from 1881 until his death in 1889.* The Library of Congress.

curing to men the blessings of civilization under the reign of just and equal laws, so that, in the famous language of the Massachusetts bill of rights, the government of the commonwealth 'may be a government of laws and not of men.' For the very idea that one man may be compelled to hold his life, or the means of living, or any material right essential to the enjoyment of life, at the mere will of another, seems to be intolerable in any country where freedom prevails, as being the essence of slavery itself. . . .

## The Administration of the Law Discriminates Illegally

In the present cases, we are not obliged to reason from the probable to the actual, and pass upon the validity of the ordinances complained of, as tried merely by the opportunities which their terms afford, of unequal and unjust discrimination in their administration; for the cases present the ordinances in actual operation, and the facts shown establish an administration directed so exclusively against a particular class of persons as to warrant and require the conclusion that, whatever may have been the intent of the ordinances as adopted, they are applied by the public authorities charged with their administration, and thus representing the state itself, with a mind so unequal and oppressive as to amount to a practical denial by the state of that equal protection of the laws which is secured to the petitioners, as to all other persons, by the broad and benign provisions of the fourteenth amendment to the constitution of the United States. Though the law itself be fair on its face, and impartial in appearance, yet, if it is applied and administered by public authority with an evil eye and an unequal hand, so as practically to make unjust and illegal discriminations between persons in similar circumstances, material to their rights, the denial of equal justice is still within the prohibition of the constitution. . . .

The present cases, as shown by the facts disclosed in the record, are within this class. It appears that both petitioners have complied with every requisite deemed by the law, or by the public officers charged with its administration, necessary for the protection of neighboring property from fire, or as a precaution against injury to the public health. No reason whatever, except the will of the supervisors, is assigned why they should not be permitted to carry on, in the accustomed manner, their harmless and useful occupation, on which they depend for a livelihood; and while this consent of the supervisors is withheld from them, and from 200 others who have also petitioned, all of whom happen to be Chinese subjects, 80 others, not Chinese subjects, are permitted to carry on the same business under similar conditions. The fact of this discrimination is admitted. No reason for it is shown, and the conclusion cannot be resisted that no reason for it exists except hostility to the race and nationality to which the petitioners belong, and which, in the eye of the law, is not justified. The discrimination is therefore illegal, and the public administration which enforces it is a denial of the equal protection of the laws, and a violation of the fourteenth amendment of the constitution. The imprisonment of the petitioners is therefore illegal, and they must be discharged. To this end the judgment of the supreme court of California in the Case of Yick Wo, and that of the circuit court of the United States for the district of California in the Case of Wo Lee, are severally reversed, and the cases remanded, each to the proper court, with directions to discharge the petitioners from custody and imprisonment.

# Racial Segregation in Public Accommodations Is Not Unconstitutional

*Henry Billings Brown*

*The following selection is an excerpt from the majority opinion in* Plessy v. Ferguson, *the now infamous Supreme Court decision that upheld the legality of racial segregation. In this opinion, Justice Henry Billings Brown expresses views that were prevalent at the time and with which all but one member of the Court agreed. Homer Plessy, who was only one-eighth black, had intentionally boarded a railroad car reserved for whites as a test of Louisiana's law mandating segregated cars. When he refused to leave, he was jailed and his case was taken to court, as planned, by a famous attorney who argued that Plessy's constitutional rights under the Fourteenth Amendment had been violated. The Supreme Court ruled that there had been no violation because there was, in its view, a clear distinction between laws concerning the political equality of blacks and those requiring the separation of races in schools, theaters, and railway carriages. The latter, it decided, were "reasonable" according to "the established usages, customs, and traditions of the people, and with a view to the promotion of their comfort, and the preservation of the public peace and good order." Moreover, the Court held that such laws did not imply that one race was inferior to the other. This decision became the basis for the "separate but equal" policy that prevailed in the South for many years, under which accommodations for blacks were rarely as equal as was claimed.*

*Henry Billings Brown, an attorney, was a justice of the U.S. Supreme Court from 1891 to 1906. He is best known today as the author of the majority opinion in* Plessy v. Ferguson.

Henry Billings Brown, majority opinion, *Plessy v. Ferguson*, U.S. Supreme Court, May 18, 1896.

The information filed in the criminal district court charged, in substance, that [Homer] Plessy, being a passenger between two stations within the state of Louisiana, was assigned by officers of the company to the coach used for the race to which he belonged, but he insisted upon going into a coach used by the race to which he did not belong. Neither in the information nor plea was his particular race or color averred [declared or verified].

The petition for the writ of prohibition averred that petitioner was seven-eights Caucasian and one-eighth African blood; that the mixture of colored blood was not discernible in him; and that he was entitled to every right, privilege, and immunity secured to citizens of the United States of the white race; and that, upon such theory, he took possession of a vacant seat in a coach where passengers of the white race were accommodated, and was ordered by the conductor to vacate said coach, and take a seat in another, assigned to persons of the colored race, and, having refused to comply with such demand, he was forcibly ejected, with the aid of a police officer, and imprisoned in the parish jail to answer a charge of having violated the above act. . . .

## The Object of the Fourteenth Amendment Was to Enforce Equality, Not to Abolish Distinctions

By the fourteenth amendment, all persons born or naturalized in the United States, and subject to the jurisdiction thereof, are made citizens of the United States and of the state wherein they reside; and the states are forbidden from making or enforcing any law which shall abridge the privileges or immunities of citizens of the United States, or shall deprive any person of life, liberty, or property without due process of law, or deny to any person within their jurisdiction the equal protection of the laws. . . .

The object of the amendment was undoubtedly to enforce the absolute equality of the two races before the law, but, in the nature of things, it could not have been intended to abolish distinctions based upon color, or to enforce social, as distinguished from political, equality, or a commingling of the two races upon terms unsatisfactory to either. Laws permitting, and even requiring, their separation, in places where they are liable to be brought into contact, do not necessarily imply the inferiority of either race to the other, and have been generally, if not universally, recognized as within the competency of the state legislatures in the exercise of their police power. The most common instance of this is connected with the establishment of separate schools for white and colored children, which have been held to be a valid exercise of the legislative power even by courts of states where the political rights of the colored race have been longest and most earnestly enforced. . . .

Laws forbidding the intermarriage of the two races may be said in a technical sense to interfere with the freedom of contract, and yet have been universally recognized as within the police power of the state.

The distinction between laws interfering with the political equality of the negro and those requiring the separation of the two races in schools, theaters, and railway carriages has been frequently drawn by this court. . . .

In the Civil Rights Cases, it was held that an act of congress entitling all persons within the jurisdiction of the United States to the full and equal enjoyment of the accommodations, advantages, facilities, and privileges of inns, public conveyances, on land or water, theaters, and other places of public amusement, and made applicable to citizens of every race and color, regardless of any previous condition of servitude, was unconstitutional and void, upon the ground that the fourteenth amendment was prohibitory upon the states only, and the legislation authorized to be adopted by congress for enforcing it was not direct legislation on matters respecting which the states were prohibited from making or enforcing certain laws, or doing certain acts, but was corrective legislation, such as might be necessary or proper for counter-acting and redressing the effect of such laws or acts. In delivering the opinion of the court, Mr. Justice [Joseph P.] Bradley observed that the fourteenth amendment 'does not invest congress with power to legislate upon subjects that are within the domain of state legislation, but to provide modes of relief against state legislation or state action of the kind referred to. It does not authorize congress to create a code of municipal law for the regulation of private rights, but to provide modes of redress against the operation of state laws, and the action of state officers, executive or judicial, when these are subversive of the fundamental rights specified in the amendment. Positive rights and privileges are undoubtedly secured by the fourteenth amendment; but they are secured by way of prohibition against state laws and state proceedings affecting those rights and privileges, and by power given to congress to legislate for the purpose of carrying such prohibition into effect; and such legislation must necessarily be predicated upon such supposed state laws or state proceedings, and be directed to the correction of their operation and effect.' ...

## Laws Requiring Separate Accommodations Must Be Reasonable

It is also suggested by the learned counsel for the plaintiff in error that the same argument that will justify the state legislature in requiring railways to provide separate accommodations for the two races will also authorize them to require separate cars to be provided for people whose hair is of a certain color, or who are aliens, or who belong to certain nationalities, or to enact laws requiring colored people to walk upon one side of the street, and white people upon the other, or requiring white men's houses to be painted white, and colored men's black, or their vehicles or business signs to be of different colors, upon the theory that one side of the street is as good as the other, or that a house or vehicle of one color is as good as one of another color. The reply to all this is that every exercise of the police power must be reasonable, and extend only to such laws as are enacted in good faith for the promotion of the public good, and not for the annoyance or oppression of a particular class. Thus, in *Yick Wo v. Hopkins*, it was held by this court that a municipal ordinance of the city of San Francisco, to regulate the carrying on of public laundries within the limits of the municipality, violated the provisions of the constitution of the United States, if it conferred upon the municipal authorities arbitrary power, at their own will, and without regard to discretion, in the legal sense of the term, to give or withhold consent as to persons or places, without regard to the competency of the persons applying or the propriety of the places selected for the carrying on of the business. It was held to be a covert attempt on the part of the municipality to make an arbitrary and unjust discrimination against the Chinese race. . . .

So far, then, as a conflict with the fourteenth amendment is concerned, the case reduces itself to the question whether the statute of Louisiana is a reasonable regulation, and with respect to this there must necessarily be a large discretion on the part of the legislature. In determining the question of reasonableness, it is at liberty to act with reference to the established usages, customs, and traditions of the people, and with a view to the promotion of their comfort, and the preservation of the public peace and good order. Gauged by this standard, we cannot say that a law which authorizes or even requires the separation of the two races in public conveyances is unreasonable, or more obnoxious to the fourteenth amendment than the acts of congress requiring separate schools for colored children in the District of Columbia, the constitutionality of which does not seem to have been questioned, or the corresponding acts of state legislatures.

## Segregation Does Not Mean Either Race Is Inferior

We consider the underlying fallacy of the plaintiff's argument to consist in the assumption that the enforced separation of the two races stamps the colored race with a badge of inferiority. If this be so, it is not by reason of anything found in the act, but solely because the colored race chooses to put that construction upon it. The argument necessarily assumes that if, as has been more than once the case, and is not unlikely to be so again, the colored race should become the dominant power in the state legislature, and should enact a law in precisely similar terms, it would thereby relegate the white race to an inferior position. We imagine that the white race, at least, would not acquiesce in this assumption. The argument also assumes that social prejudices may be overcome by legislation, and that equal rights cannot be secured to the negro except by an enforced commingling of the two races. We cannot accept this proposition. If the two races are to meet upon terms of social equality, it must be the result of natural affinities, a mutual appreciation of each other's merits, and a voluntary consent of individuals. . . . Legislation is powerless to eradicate racial instincts, or to abolish distinctions based upon physical differences, and the attempt to do so can only result in accentuating the difficulties of the present situation. If the civil and political rights of both races be equal, one cannot be inferior to the other civilly or politically. If one race be inferior to the other socially, the constitution of the United States cannot put them upon the same plane.

# Under the Constitution Racial Segregation Cannot Be Tolerated

*John Marshall Harlan*

*Justice John Marshall Harlan's dissent in* Plessy v. Ferguson, *portions of which follow, is one of the best-known opinions in Supreme Court history. In it, Harlan argues that although a Louisiana law requiring separate accommodations for blacks and whites in railroad cars pretended to apply equally to both races, everyone knew that its real purpose was to exclude blacks from accommodations used by whites—a purpose, in his view, not sanctioned by the Constitution. "The Constitution is color-blind," he wrote, coining a phrase that has become famous. In Harlan's opinion, the Court's decision that the Fourteenth Amendment had not been violated by Louisiana's law would, "in time, prove to be quite as pernicious as the decision made by this tribunal in the Dred Scott Case" (an 1857 case in which the Court ruled that people of African descent were not citizens of the United States). This prediction proved to be correct with respect to the views that have prevailed since the late twentieth century.*

*John Marshall Harlan was a justice of the U.S. Supreme Court from 1877 until 1911. He was known as "the great dissenter" because he often disagreed forcefully with the majority. Harlan was born into a Kentucky slave-owning family and supported slavery during the Civil War, although he fought to preserve the Union. Later, dismayed by the terrorist activities of the Ku Klux Klan, he turned strongly against slavery and became a champion of civil rights for blacks.*

John Marshall Harlan, dissenting opinion, *Plessy v. Ferguson*, U.S. Supreme Court, May 18, 1896.

In respect of civil rights, common to all citizens, the constitution of the United States does not, I think, permit any public authority to know the race of those entitled to be protected in the enjoyment of such rights. Every true man has pride of race, and under appropriate circumstances, when the rights of others, his equals before the law, are not to be affected, it is his privilege to express such pride and to take such action based upon it as to him seems proper. But I deny that any legislative body or judicial tribunal may have regard to the race of citizens when the civil rights of those citizens are involved. Indeed, such legislation as that here in question is inconsistent not only with that equality of rights which pertains to citizenship, national and state, but with the personal liberty enjoyed by every one within the United States. . . .

[The thirteenth] amendment having been found inadequate to the protection of the rights of those who had been in slavery, it was followed by the fourteenth amendment, which added greatly to the dignity and glory of American citizenship, and to the security of personal liberty, by declaring that 'all persons born or naturalized in the United States, and subject to the jurisdiction thereof, are citizens of the United States and of the state wherein they reside,' and that 'no state shall make or enforce any law which shall abridge the privileges or immunities of citizens of the United States; nor shall any state deprive any person of life, liberty or property without due process of law, nor deny to any person within its jurisdiction the equal protection of the laws.' These two amendments, if enforced according to their true intent and meaning, will protect all the civil rights that pertain to freedom and citizenship. . . .

These notable additions to the fundamental law were welcomed by the friends of liberty throughout the world. They removed the race line from our governmental systems. . . .

# The Law Was Intended to Exclude Blacks from White Railroad Cars

It was said in argument that the statute of Louisiana does not discriminate against either race, but prescribes a rule applicable alike to white and colored citizens. But this argument does not meet the difficulty. Every one knows that the statute in question had its origin in the purpose, not so much to exclude white persons from railroad cars occupied by blacks, as to exclude colored people from coaches occupied by or assigned to white persons. Railroad corporations of Louisiana did not make discrimination among whites in the matter of commodation for travelers. The thing to accomplish was, under the guise of giving equal accommodation for whites and blacks, to compel the latter to keep to themselves while traveling in railroad passenger coaches. No one would be so wanting in candor as to assert the contrary. The fundamental objection, therefore, to the statute, is that it interferes with the personal freedom of citizens. 'Personal liberty,' it has been well said, 'consists in the power of locomotion, of changing situation, or removing one's person to whatsoever places one's own inclination may direct, without imprisonment or restraint, unless by due course of law.' If a white man and a black man choose to occupy the same public conveyance on a public highway, it is their right to do so; and no government, proceeding alone on grounds of race, can prevent it without infringing the personal liberty of each. . . .

If a state can prescribe, as a rule of civil conduct, that whites and blacks shall not travel as passengers in the same railroad coach, why may it not so regulate the use of the streets of its cities and towns as to compel white citizens to keep on one side of a street, and black citizens to keep on the other? Why may it not, upon like grounds, punish whites and blacks who ride together in street cars or in open vehicles on a public road or street? Why may it not require sheriffs to assign whites to one side of a court room, and blacks to the other? And why may it not also prohibit the commingling of the two races in the galleries of legislative halls or in public assemblages convened for the consideration of the political questions of the day? Further, if this statute of Louisiana is consistent with the personal liberty of citizens, why may not the state require the separation in railroad coaches of native and naturalized citizens of the United States, or of Protestants and Roman Catholics?. . .

## The Constitution Is Color-Blind

The white race deems itself to be the dominant race in this country. And so it is, in prestige, in achievements, in education, in wealth, and in power. So, I doubt not, it will continue to be for all time, if it remains true to its great heritage, and holds fast to the principles of constitutional liberty. But in view of the constitution, in the eye of the law, there is in this country no superior, dominant, ruling class of citizens. There is no caste here. Our constitution is color-blind, and neither knows nor tolerates classes among citizens. In respect of civil rights, all citizens are equal before the law. The humblest is the peer of the most powerful. The law regards man as man, and takes no account of his surroundings or of his color when his civil rights as guarantied by the supreme law of the land are involved. It is therefore to be regretted that this high tribunal, the final expositor of the fundamental law of the land, has reached the conclusion that it is competent for a state to regulate the enjoyment by citizens of their civil rights solely upon the basis of race.

In my opinion, the judgment this day rendered will, in time, prove to be quite as pernicious as the decision made by this tribunal in the Dred Scott Case.

It was adjudged in that case that the descendants of Africans who were imported into this country, and sold as slaves, were not included nor intended to be included under the word 'citizens' in the constitution, and could not claim any of the rights and privileges which that instrument provided for and secured to citizens of the United States; that, at time of the adoption of the constitution, they were 'considered as a subordinate and inferior class of beings, who had been subjugated by the dominant race, and, whether emancipated or not, yet remained subject to their authority, and had no rights or privileges but such as those who held the power and the government might choose to grant them.' The recent amendments of the constitution, it was supposed, had eradicated these principles from our institutions. But it seems that we have yet, in some of the states, a dominant race—a superior class of citizens—which assumes to regulate the enjoyment of civil rights, common to all citizens, upon the basis of race. The present decision, it may well be apprehended, will not only stimulate aggressions, more or less brutal and irritating, upon the admitted rights of colored citizens, but will encourage the belief that it is possible, by means of state enactments, to defeat the beneficent purposes which the people of the United States had in view when they adopted the recent amendments of the constitution, by one of which the blacks of this country were made citizens of the United States and of the states in which they respectively reside, and whose privileges and immunities, as citizens, the states are forbidden to abridge. Sixty millions of whites are in no danger from the presence here of eight millions of blacks. The destinies of the two races, in this country, are indissolubly linked together, and the interests of both require that the common government of all shall not permit the seeds of race hate to be planted under the sanction of law. What can more certainly arouse race hate, what more certainly create and perpetuate a feeling of distrust between these races, than state enactments which, in fact, proceed on the ground that colored citizens are so inferior and degraded that they cannot be allowed to sit in public coaches occupied by white citizens? That, as all will admit, is the real meaning of such legislation as was enacted in Louisiana.

## Segregation by Race Cannot Be
## Justified and Will Do Great Harm

The sure guaranty of the peace and security of each race is the clear, distinct, unconditional recognition by our governments, national and state, of every right that inheres in civil freedom, and of the equality before the law of all citizens of the United States, without regard to race. State enactments regulating the enjoyment of civil rights upon the basis of race, and cunningly devised to defeat legitimate results of the war, under the pretense of recognizing equality of rights, can have no other result than to render permanent peace impossible, and to keep alive a conflict of races, the continuance of which must do harm to all concerned. . . .

By the statute in question, a Chinaman can ride in the same passenger coach with white citizens of the United States, while citizens of the black race in Louisiana, many of whom, perhaps, risked their lives for the preservation of the Union, who are entitled, by law, to participate in the political control of the state and nation, who are not excluded, by law or by reason of their race, from public stations of any kind, and who have all the legal rights that belong to white citizens, are yet declared to be criminals, liable to imprisonment, if they ride in a public coach occupied by citizens of the white race. It is scarcely just to say that a colored citizen should not object to occupying a public coach assigned to his own race. He does not object, nor, perhaps, would he object to separate coaches for his race if his rights under the law were recognized. But he does object, and he ought never to cease objecting, that citizens of the white and black races can be adjudged criminals because they sit, or claim the right to sit, in the same public coach on a public highway. The arbitrary separation of citizens, on the basis of race, while they are on a public highway, is a badge of servitude wholly inconsistent with the civil freedom and the equality before the law established by the constitution. It cannot be justified upon any legal grounds.

If evils will result from the commingling of the two races upon public highways established for the benefit of all, they will be infinitely less than those that will surely come from state legislation regulating the enjoyment of civil rights upon the basis of race. We boast of the freedom enjoyed by our people above all other peoples. But it is difficult to reconcile that boast with a state of the law which, practically, puts the brand of servitude and degradation upon a large class of our fellow citizens—our equals before the law. The thin disguise of 'equal' accommodations for passengers in railroad coaches will not mislead any one, nor atone for the wrong this day done.

# Racial Segregation in Public Education Is Unconstitutional

*Earl Warren*

*One of the most significant and far-reaching of the Supreme Court's decisions interpreting the Fourteenth Amendment was that handed down in* Brown v. Board of Education. *In that landmark decision, the Court overturned its 1896 ruling in* Plessy v. Ferguson, *declaring that the segregation of blacks and whites in public schools was unconstitutional under the Equal Protection Clause of the Fourteenth Amendment. This case combined five cases from different states that were decided together. In all of them, parents had attempted to enroll their black children in schools reserved for whites but had been turned away. The named plaintiff, Oliver Brown, was the father of Linda Brown, a third-grade girl who became a "poster child" representing about two hundred others. In her particular instance, unlike most, the black school that she was required to attend was found to be of equal quality. However, the Court ruled that in the modern era, the mere fact of segregation had a detrimental effect on the education of black children. "We cannot turn the clock back to 1868 when the Amendment was adopted, or even to 1896 when* Plessy v. Ferguson *was written," Chief Justice Earl Warren wrote. This decision was discussed over a period of more than a year until the justices agreed to make it unanimous, for the Court knew that it would be extremely controversial and would be resisted by the Southern states. Desegregation proved to be a slow process.*

*Earl Warren was the chief justice of the U.S. Supreme Court from 1953 to 1969. Before taking the bench he served three terms as governor of California and ran as the Republican nominee for vice president of the United States in the 1948 election.*

Earl Warren, unanimous opinion, *Brown v. Board of Education*, U.S. Supreme Court, May 17, 1954.

*He was one of the most influential Supreme Court justices in U.S. history, but also among the most controversial. During Warren's tenure as chief justice, the Court made many decisions that expanded the meaning of the Fourteenth Amendment and had a direct impact on American life.*

The plaintiffs contend that segregated public schools are not "equal" and cannot be made "equal," and that hence they are deprived of the equal protection of the laws. Because of the obvious importance of the question presented, the Court took jurisdiction. Argument was heard in the 1952 Term, and reargument was heard this Term on certain questions propounded by the Court.

Reargument was largely devoted to the circumstances surrounding the adoption of the Fourteenth Amendment in 1868. It covered exhaustively consideration of the Amendment in Congress, ratification by the states, then existing practices in racial segregation, and the views of proponents and opponents of the Amendment. This discussion and our own investigation convince us that, although these sources cast some light, it is not enough to resolve the problem with which we are faced. At best, they are inconclusive. The most avid proponents of the post-War Amendments undoubtedly intended them to remove all legal distinctions among "all persons born or naturalized in the United States." Their opponents, just as certainly, were antagonistic to both the letter and the spirit of the Amendments and wished them to have the most limited effect. What others in Congress and the state legislatures had in mind cannot be determined with any degree of certainty.

An additional reason for the inconclusive nature of the Amendment's history, with respect to segregated schools, is the status of public education at that time. In the South, the movement toward free common schools, supported by general taxation, had not yet taken hold. Education of white children was largely in the hands of private groups. Education of Negroes was almost nonexistent, and practically all of the race were illiterate. In fact, any education of Negroes was forbidden by law in some states. Today, in contrast, many Negroes have achieved outstanding success in the arts and sciences as well as in the business and professional world. It is true that public school education at the time of the Amendment had advanced further in the North, but the effect of the Amendment on Northern States was generally ignored in the congressional debates. Even in the North, the conditions of public education did not approximate those existing today. The curriculum was usually rudimentary; ungraded schools were common in rural areas; the school term was but three months a year in many states; and compulsory school attendance was virtually unknown. As a consequence, it is not surprising that there should be so little in the history of the Fourteenth Amendment relating to its intended effect on public education.

In the first cases in this Court construing the Fourteenth Amendment, decided shortly after its adoption, the Court interpreted it as proscribing all state-imposed discriminations against the Negro race. The doctrine of "separate but equal" did not make its appearance in this Court until 1896 in the case of *Plessy v. Ferguson*, involving not education but transportation. American courts have since labored with the doctrine for over half a century. In this Court, there have been six cases involving the "separate but equal" doctrine in the field of public education.... In none of these cases was it necessary to re-examine the doctrine to grant relief to the Negro plaintiff. And in *Sweatt v. Painter*, the Court expressly reserved decision on the question whether *Plessy v. Ferguson* should be held inapplicable to public education.

## Segregation Deprives Minorities of Equal Educational Opportunities

In the instant [present] cases, that question is directly presented. Here, unlike *Sweatt v. Painter*, there are findings below that the Negro and white schools involved have been equalized, or are being equalized, with respect to buildings, curricula, qualifications and salaries of teachers, and other "tangible" factors. Our decision, therefore, cannot turn on merely a comparison of these tangible factors in the Negro and white schools involved in each of the cases. We must look instead to the effect of segregation itself on public education.

In approaching this problem, we cannot turn the clock back to 1868 when the Amendment was adopted, or even to 1896 when *Plessy v. Ferguson* was written. We must consider public education in the light of its full development and its present place in American life throughout the Nation. Only in this way can it be determined if segregation in public schools deprives these plaintiffs of the equal protection of the laws.

Today, education is perhaps the most important function of state and local governments. Compulsory school attendance laws and the great expenditures for education both demonstrate our recognition of the importance of education to our democratic society. It is required in the performance of our most basic public responsibilities, even service in the armed forces. It is the very foundation of good citizenship. Today it is a principal instrument in awakening the child to cultural values, in preparing him for later professional training, and in helping him to adjust normally to his environment. In these days, it is doubtful that any child may reasonably be expected to succeed in life if he is denied the opportunity of an education. Such an opportunity, where the state has undertaken to provide it, is a right which must be made available to all on equal terms.

We come then to the question presented: Does segregation of children in public schools solely on the basis of race, even though the physical facilities and other "tangible" factors may be equal, deprive the children of the minority group of equal educational opportunities? We believe that it does. . . .

To separate [children] from others of similar age and qualifications solely because of their race generates a feeling of inferiority as to their status in the community that may affect their hearts and minds in a way unlikely ever to be undone. The effect of this separation on their educational opportunities was well stated by a finding in the Kansas cases [one of the cases being decided] by a court which nevertheless felt compelled to rule against the Negro plaintiffs:

"Segregation of white and colored children in public schools has a detrimental effect upon the colored children. The impact is greater when it has the sanction of the law; for the policy of separating the races is usually interpreted as denoting the inferiority of the negro group. A sense of inferiority affects the motivation of a child to learn. Segregation with the sanction of law, therefore, has a tendency to [retard] the educational and mental development of negro children and to deprive them of some of the benefits they would receive in a racial[ly] integrated school system."

Whatever may have been the extent of psychological knowledge at the time of *Plessy v. Ferguson*, this finding is amply supported by modern authority. Any language in *Plessy v. Ferguson* contrary to this finding is rejected.

We conclude that in the field of public education the doctrine of "separate but equal" has no place. Separate educational facilities are inherently unequal. Therefore, we hold that the plaintiffs and others similarly situated for whom the actions have been brought are, by reason of the segregation complained of, deprived of the equal protection of the laws guaranteed by the Fourteenth Amendment.

# Race Cannot Be Used as a Basis for School Admission, Even to Achieve Diversity

*John Roberts*

*The following selection is excerpted from Chief Justice John Roberts's presentation of the Supreme Court's opinion in the 2007 case* Parents Involved in Community Schools v. Seattle School District, *which was, and still is, extremely controversial. Portions of it represent a plurality opinion rather than a majority opinion, which means that a majority of the Court's members did not assent to those sections—in this case the justices disagreed sharply and many separate opinions were written.* Parents v. Seattle *was decided along with another case involving Jefferson County, Kentucky. The Court ruled 5–4 that school districts cannot use race as a factor in assigning students to schools, even when the aim is to achieve racial balance. Seattle students who wanted to change schools could apply to the schools they preferred, but if there was not room for all the applicants, those of minority races had preference. Since the end of school segregation, similar methods of compensating for past injustices have become common in many localities, and some people believe that this is a justifiable form of unequal treatment. However, others believe that it merely perpetuates racial distinctions and that, under the Equal Protection Clause, race should not be considered for any reason. "The way to stop discrimination on the basis of race," writes Chief Justice Roberts, "is to stop discriminating on the basis of race."*

*John Roberts became the chief justice of the U.S. Supreme Court in 2005. Previously he had been a judge on the U.S. Court of Appeals for the District of Columbia. He is a conservative jurist who believes in interpreting the Constitution strictly.*

John Roberts, plurality opinion, *Parents Involved in Community Schools v. Seattle School District*, U.S. Supreme Court, June 28, 2007.

Seattle contends that its use of race helps to reduce racial concentration in schools and to ensure that racially concentrated housing patterns do not prevent nonwhite students from having access to the most desirable schools. Jefferson County has articulated a similar goal, phrasing its interest in terms of educating its students "in a racially integrated environment." Each school district argues that educational and broader socialization benefits flow from a racially diverse learning environment, and each contends that because the diversity they seek is racial diversity—not the broader diversity at issue in *Grutter* [*Grutter v. Bollinger*, 2003]—it makes sense to promote that interest directly by relying on race alone.

The parties and their *amici* [friends of the court] dispute whether racial diversity in schools in fact has a marked impact on test scores and other objective yardsticks or achieves intangible socialization benefits. The debate is not one we need to resolve, however, because it is clear that the racial classifications employed by the districts are not narrowly tailored to the goal of achieving the educational and social benefits asserted to flow from racial diversity. In design and operation, the plans are directed only to racial balance, pure and simple, an objective this Court has repeatedly condemned as illegitimate. . . .

Accepting racial balancing as a compelling state interest would justify the imposition of racial proportionality throughout American society, contrary to our repeated recognition that "[a]t the heart of the Constitution's guarantee of equal protection lies the simple command that the Government must treat citizens as individuals, not as simply components of a racial, religious, sexual or national class" [*Miller v. Johnson*, 1995, quoting *Metro Broadcasting v. FCC*, 1990, dissenting opinion of Justice Sandra Day O'Connor]. Allowing racial balancing as a compelling end in itself would "effectively assur[e] that race will always be relevant in American life, and that the 'ultimate goal' of 'eliminating entirely from governmental de-

*Chief Justice of the Supreme Court John Roberts. Justice Roberts was appointed to the Supreme Court in 2005.* AP Images.

cisionmaking such irrelevant factors as a human being's race'
will never be achieved" [*Richmond v. J.A. Croson*, 1989, plurality opinion of Justice O'Connor]. An interest "linked to nothing other than proportional representation of various races
... would support indefinite use of racial classifications, em-

ployed first to obtain the appropriate mixture of racial views and then to ensure that the [program] continues to reflect that mixture"[ *Metro Broadcasting*, dissenting opinion of Justice O'Connor]. . . .

The principle that racial balancing is not permitted is one of substance, not semantics. Racial balancing is not transformed from "patently unconstitutional" to a compelling state interest simply by relabeling it "racial diversity." While the school districts use various verbal formulations to describe the interest they seek to promote—racial diversity, avoidance of racial isolation, racial integration—they offer no definition of the interest that suggests it differs from racial balance. . . .

The en banc Ninth Circuit [the decision being reviewed] declared that "when a racially diverse school system is the goal (or racial concentration or isolation is the problem), there is no more effective means than a consideration of race to achieve the solution." For the foregoing reasons, this conclusory argument cannot sustain the plans. However closely related race-based assignments may be to achieving racial balance, that itself cannot be the goal, whether labeled "racial diversity" or anything else. To the extent the objective is sufficient diversity so that students see fellow students as individuals rather than solely as members of a racial group, using means that treat students solely as members of a racial group is fundamentally at cross-purposes with that end. . . .

## The Dissenting Arguments Are Not Valid

Justice [Stephen] Breyer [in his dissenting opinion] seeks to justify the plans at issue under our precedents recognizing the compelling interest in remedying past intentional discrimination. Not even the school districts go this far, and for good reason. The distinction between segregation by state action and racial imbalance caused by other factors has been central to our jurisprudence in this area for generations. The dissent elides this distinction between *de jure* [legal] and *de facto* [actual] segregation, casually intimates that Seattle's school attendance patterns reflect illegal segregation, and fails to credit the judicial determination—under the most rigorous standard—that Jefferson County had eliminated the vestiges of prior segregation. The dissent thus alters in fundamental ways not only the facts presented here but the established law. . . .

Justice Breyer speaks of bringing "the races" together (putting aside the purely black-and-white nature of the plans), as the justification for excluding individuals on the basis of their race. Again, this approach to racial classifications is fundamentally at odds with our precedent, which makes clear that the Equal Protection Clause "protect[s] *persons*, not *groups*" [*Adarand Constructors v. Mineta*, 2001, emphasis in original]. . . .

Justice Breyer's position comes down to a familiar claim: The end justifies the means. He admits that "there is a cost in applying 'a state-mandated racial label,'" but he is confident that the cost is worth paying. Our established strict scrutiny test for racial classifications, however, insists on "detailed examination, both as to ends *and* as to means" [*Adarand*, emphasis added]. Simply because the school districts may seek a worthy goal does not mean they are free to discriminate on the basis of race to achieve it, or that their racial classifications should be subject to less exacting scrutiny. . . .

We employ the familiar and well-established analytic approach of strict scrutiny to evaluate the plans at issue today, an approach that in no way warrants the dissent's cataclysmic concerns. Under that approach, the school districts have not carried their burden of showing that the ends they seek justify the particular extreme means they have chosen—classifying individual students on the basis of their race and discriminating among them on that basis.

# Race Cannot Be Used to Discriminate in Education

If the need for the racial classifications embraced by the school districts is unclear, even on the districts' own terms, the costs are undeniable. "[D]istinctions between citizens solely because of their ancestry are by their very nature odious to a free people whose institutions are founded upon the doctrine of equality" [*Adarand*]. Government action dividing us by race is inherently suspect because such classifications promote "notions of racial inferiority and lead to a politics of racial hostility" [*Croson*], "reinforce the belief, held by too many for too much of our history, that individuals should be judged by the color of their skin" [*Shaw v. Reno*, 1993], and "endorse race-based reasoning and the conception of a Nation divided into racial blocs, thus contributing to an escalation of racial hostility and conflict" [*Metro Broadcasting*, dissenting opinion of Justice O'Connor]. As the Court explained in *Rice v. Cayetano*, "[o]ne of the principal reasons race is treated as a forbidden classification is that it demeans the dignity and worth of a person to be judged by ancestry instead of by his or her own merit and essential qualities.". . .

The parties and their *amici* debate which side is more faithful to the heritage of *Brown* [*Brown v. Board of Education*, 1954], but the position of the plaintiffs in *Brown* was spelled out in their brief and could not have been clearer: "[T]he Fourteenth Amendment prevents states from according differential treatment to American children on the basis of their color of race." What do the racial classifications at issue here do, if not accord differential treatment on the basis of race? As counsel who appeared before this Court for the plaintiffs in *Brown* put it: "We have one fundamental contention which we will seek to develop in the course of this argument, and that contention is that no State has any authority under the equal-protection clause of the Fourteenth Amendment to use race as a factor in affording educational opportunities among its citizens." There is no ambiguity in that statement. And it was that position that prevailed in this Court, which emphasized in its remedial opinion that what was "[a]t stake is the personal interest of the plaintiffs in admission to public schools as soon as practicable *on a nondiscriminatory basis*," and what was required was "determining admission to the public schools *on a nonracial basis*" [*Brown v. Board of Education II*, emphasis added]. What do the racial classifications do in these cases, if not determine admission to a public school on a racial basis? Before *Brown*, schoolchildren were told where they could and could not go to school based on the color of their skin. The school districts in these cases have not carried the heavy burden of demonstrating that we should allow this once again—even for very different reasons. For schools that never segregated on the basis of race, such as Seattle, or that have removed the vestiges of past segregation, such as Jefferson County, the way "to achieve a system of determining admission to the public schools on a nonracial basis" [*Brown II*], is to stop assigning students on a racial basis. The way to stop discrimination on the basis of race is to stop discriminating on the basis of race.

# Affirmative Action in School Integration Does Not Violate the Fourteenth Amendment

*Stephen Breyer*

*The following selection is the concluding portion of Supreme Court Justice Stephen Breyer's dissenting opinion in* Parents Involved in Community Schools v. Seattle School District, *in which he was joined by three other justices. In statements sharply critical of the Court's decision, Breyer summarizes his long and detailed discussion of the history of school segregation and the methods that have been used to combat it. He states that the law has always upheld these methods and that they have not previously been held to be unconstitutional under the Equal Protection Clause of the Fourteenth Amendment. That clause, he writes, "has always distinguished in practice between state action that excludes and thereby subordinates racial minorities and state action that seeks to bring together people of all races." In Breyer's view, such action is necessary to undo the harm caused by segregation. He believes that the Court's ruling conflicts with the ideals established by* Brown v. Board of Education *and that it will set back efforts to achieve racial equality. Moreover, he says, by making existing practices unlawful, it will lead to legal uncertainty and further litigation. He considers it a decision that the nation will come to regret.*

*Stephen Breyer has been a justice of the U. S. Supreme Court since 1994. He is liberal in his approach to constitutional law, which means that he believes the Constitution should be interpreted in light of modern conditions.*

Stephen Breyer, dissenting opinion, *Parents Involved in Community Schools v. Seattle School District*, U.S. Supreme Court, June 28, 2007.

To show that the school assignment plans here meet the requirements of the Constitution, I have written at exceptional length. But that length is necessary. I cannot refer to the history of the plans in these cases to justify the use of race-conscious criteria without describing that history in full. I cannot rely upon *Swann*'s [*Swann v. Charlotte-Mecklenburg Board of Education*, 1971] statement that the use of race-conscious limits is permissible without showing, rather than simply asserting, that the statement represents a constitutional principle firmly rooted in federal and state law. Nor can I explain my disagreement with the Court's holding and the plurality's opinion [the opinion giving the Court's decision] without offering a detailed account of the arguments they propound and the consequences they risk.

Thus, the opinion's reasoning is long. But its conclusion is short: The plans before us satisfy the requirements of the Equal Protection Clause. And it is the plurality's opinion, not this dissent that "fails to ground the result it would reach in law."

Four basic considerations have led me to this view. *First*, the histories of Louisville and Seattle reveal complex circumstances and a long tradition of conscientious efforts by local school boards to resist racial segregation in public schools. Segregation at the time of *Brown* gave way to expansive remedies that included busing, which in turn gave rise to fears of white flight and resegregation. For decades now, these school boards have considered and adopted and revised assignment plans that sought to rely less upon race, to emphasize greater student choice, and to improve the conditions of all schools for all students, no matter the color of their skin, no matter where they happen to reside. The plans under review—which are less burdensome, more egalitarian, and more effective than prior plans—continue in that tradition. And their history reveals school district goals whose remedial, educational, and democratic elements are inextricably intertwined each with the others.

| Black Students in Segregated Schools | | | | | | | | | |
|---|---|---|---|---|---|---|---|---|---|
| *Percentage of Black Students in 90–100 Percent Nonwhite and Majority Nonwhite Public Schools by Region, 1950–1954 to 2000, Fall Enrollment* | | | | | | | | | |
| Region | 1950–1954 | 1960–1961 | 1968 | 1972 | 1976 | 1980 | 1989 | 1999 | 2000 |
| | | | Percentage in 90–100% Nonwhite Schools | | | | | | |
| Northeast | — | 40 | 42.7 | 46.9 | 51.4 | 48.7 | 49.8 | 50.2 | 51.2 |
| Border | 100 | 59 | 60.2 | 54.7 | 42.5 | 37.0 | 33.7 | 39.7 | 39.6 |
| South | 100 | 100 | 77.8 | 24.7 | 22.4 | 23.0 | 26.0 | 31.1 | 30.9 |
| Midwest | 53 | 56 | 58.0 | 57.4 | 51.1 | 43.6 | 40.1 | 45.0 | 46.3 |
| West | — | 27 | 50.8 | 42.7 | 36.3 | 33.7 | 26.7 | 29.9 | 29.5 |
| U.S. continued | | | 64.3 | 38.7 | 35.9 | 33.2 | 33.8 | 37.4 | 37.4 |

*Second*, since this Court's decision in *Brown*, the law has consistently and unequivocally approved of both voluntary and compulsory race-conscious measures to combat segregated schools. The Equal Protection Clause, ratified following the Civil War, has always distinguished in practice between state action that excludes and thereby subordinates racial minorities and state action that seeks to bring together people of all races. From *Swann* to *Grutter* [*Grutter v. Bollinger*, 2003], this Court's decisions have emphasized this distinction, recognizing that the fate of race relations in this country depends upon unity among our children, "for unless our children begin to learn together, there is little hope that our people will ever learn to live together" [*Milliken v. Bradley*, 1974, dissenting opinion of Justice Thurgood Marshall].

*Third*, the plans before us, subjected to rigorous judicial review, are supported by compelling state interests and are narrowly tailored to accomplish those goals. Just as diversity in higher education was deemed compelling in *Grutter*, diversity in public primary and secondary schools—where there is even more to gain—must be, *a fortiori* [even more], a compelling state interest. Even apart from *Grutter*, five Members of this Court agree that "avoiding racial isolation" and "achiev[ing] a diverse student population" remain today compelling interests. These interests combine remedial, educational, and democratic objectives. For the reasons discussed above, however, I disagree with Justice Kennedy that Seattle and Louis-

**Black Students in Segregated Schools** [CONTINUED]

*Percentage of Black Students in 90–100 Percent Nonwhite and Majority Nonwhite Public Schools by Region, 1950–1954 to 2000, Fall Enrollment*

| Region | 1950–1954 | 1960–1961 | 1968 | 1972 | 1976 | 1980 | 1989 | 1999 | 2000 |
|---|---|---|---|---|---|---|---|---|---|
| | | | Percentage in 50–100% Nonwhite Schools | | | | | | |
| Northeast | — | 62 | 66.8 | 69.9 | 72.5 | 79.9 | 75.4 | 77.5 | 78.3 |
| Border | 100 | 69 | 71.6 | 67.2 | 60.1 | 59.2 | 58.0 | 64.8 | 67.0 |
| South | 100 | 100 | 80.9 | 55.3 | 54.9 | 57.1 | 59.3 | 67.3 | 69.0 |
| Midwest | 78 | 80 | 77.3 | 75.3 | 70.3 | 69.5 | 69.4 | 67.9 | 73.3 |
| West | — | 69 | 72.2 | 68.1 | 67.4 | 66.8 | 67.4 | 76.7 | 75.3 |
| U.S. | — | | 76.6 | 63.6 | 62.4 | 62.9 | 64.9 | 70.1 | 71.6 |

TAKEN FROM: Appendix to Stephen Breyer dissenting opinion, *Parents v. Leattee*, C. Clotfelter, After *Brown*: The Rise and Retreat of School Desegregation 56 (2004) (Table 2.1).

ville have not done enough to demonstrate that their present plans are necessary to continue upon the path set by *Brown*. These plans are *more* "narrowly tailored" than the race-conscious law school admissions criteria at issue in *Grutter*. Hence, their lawfulness *a fortiori* follows from this Court's prior decisions.

# The Court's Decision Sets Back Local Efforts to Bring About Racially Diverse Schools

*Fourth*, the plurality's approach risks serious harm to the law and for the Nation. Its view of the law rests either upon a denial of the distinction between exclusionary and inclusive use of race-conscious criteria in the context of the Equal Protection Clause, or upon such a rigid application of its "test" that the distinction loses practical significance. Consequently, the Court's decision today slows down and sets back the work of local school boards to bring about racially diverse schools.

Indeed, the consequences of the approach the Court takes today are serious. Yesterday, the plans under review were lawful. Today, they are not. Yesterday, the citizens of this Nation could look for guidance to this Court's unanimous pronouncements concerning desegregation. Today, they cannot. Yesterday, school boards had available to them a full range of means to combat segregated schools. Today, they do not.

The Court's decision undermines other basic institutional principles as well. What has happened to *stare decisis* [the principle that precedents set by previous cases should be followed]? The history of the plans before us, their educational importance, their highly limited use of race—all these and more—make clear that the compelling interest here is stronger than in *Grutter*. The plans here are more narrowly tailored than the law school admissions program there at issue. Hence, applying *Grutter*'s strict test, their lawfulness follows *a fortiori*. To hold to the contrary is to transform that test from "strict" to "fatal in fact"—the very opposite of what *Grutter* said. And what has happened to *Swann*? To *McDaniel*? To *Crawford*? To *Harris*? To *School Committee of Boston*? To *Seattle School Dist. No.1*? After decades of vibrant life, they would all, under the plurality's logic, be written out of the law.

And what of respect for democratic local decisionmaking by States and school boards? For several decades this Court has rested its public school decisions upon *Swann*'s basic view that the Constitution grants local school districts a significant degree of leeway where the inclusive use of race-conscious criteria is at issue. Now localities will have to cope with the difficult problems they face (including resegregation) deprived of one means they may find necessary.

And what of law's concern to diminish and peacefully settle conflict among the Nation's people? Instead of accommodating different good-faith visions of our country and our Constitution, today's holding upsets settled expectations, creates legal uncertainty, and threatens to produce considerable further litigation, aggravating race-related conflict.

And what of the long history and moral vision that the Fourteenth Amendment itself embodies? The plurality cites in support those who argued in *Brown* against segregation, and *Justice [Clarence] Thomas* likens the approach that I have taken to that of segregation's defenders. But segregation policies did not simply tell schoolchildren "where they could and could not go to school based on the color of their skin," they perpetuated a caste system rooted in the institutions of slavery and 80 years of legalized subordination. The lesson of history is not that efforts to continue racial segregation are constitutionally indistinguishable from efforts to achieve racial integration. Indeed, it is a cruel distortion of history to compare Topeka, Kansas, in the 1950's to Louisville and Seattle in the modern day—to equate the plight of Linda Brown (who was ordered to attend a Jim Crow school) to the circumstances of Joshua McDonald (whose request to transfer to a school closer to home was initially declined). This is not to deny that there is a cost in applying "a state-mandated racial label." But that cost does not approach, in degree or in kind, the terrible harms of slavery, the resulting caste system, and 80 years of legal racial segregation.

## The Court's Decision Threatens Progress in Racial Equality

Finally, what of the hope and promise of *Brown*? For much of this Nation's history, the races remained divided. It was not long ago that people of different races drank from separate fountains, rode on separate buses, and studied in separate schools. In this Court's finest hour, *Brown v. Board of Education* challenged this history and helped to change it. For *Brown* held out a promise. It was a promise embodied in three Amendments designed to make citizens of slaves. It was the promise of true racial equality—not as a matter of fine words on paper, but as a matter of everyday life in the Nation's cities and schools. It was about the nature of a democracy that must work for all Americans. It sought one law, one Nation, one people, not simply as a matter of legal principle but in terms of how we actually live.

Not everyone welcomed this Court's decision in *Brown*. Three years after that decision was handed down, the Governor of Arkansas ordered state militia to block the doors of a white schoolhouse so that black children could not enter. The President of the United States dispatched the 101st Airborne Division to Little Rock, Arkansas, and federal troops were needed to enforce a desegregation decree. Today, almost 50 years later, attitudes toward race in this Nation have changed dramatically. Many parents, white and black alike, want their children to attend schools with children of different races. Indeed, the very school districts that once spurned integration now strive for it. The long history of their efforts reveals the complexities and difficulties they have faced. And in light of those challenges, they have asked us not to take from their hands the instruments they have used to rid their schools of racial segregation, instruments that they believe are needed to overcome the problems of cities divided by race and poverty. The plurality would decline their modest request.

The plurality is wrong to do so. The last half-century has witnessed great strides toward racial equality, but we have not yet realized the promise of *Brown*. To invalidate the plans under review is to threaten the promise of *Brown*. The plurality's position, I fear, would break that promise. This is a decision that the Court and the Nation will come to regret.

# CHAPTER 3

# Equal Protection for Women, Immigrants, and Gays

# Laws That Discriminate on the Basis of Gender Are Unconstitutional

*Warren Burger*

*The following selection is excerpted from the opinion written by Supreme Court Chief Justice Warren Burger in the 1971 case of Reed v. Reed. This was not a controversial case and the decision was unanimous, but it is considered a landmark because it was the first case in which the Court ruled that discrimination against women violates the Equal Protection Clause of the Constitution's Fourteenth Amendment. The point at issue was who should be appointed to administer the estate of someone who dies without a will. When Richard Lynn Reed died at the age of sixteen, his divorced parents both wanted to be the administrator. The probate court (a local court in charge of settling the affairs of deceased persons) chose the father because of a state law that said men should be chosen over women in case of a conflict. The mother, Sally Reed, appealed to the Idaho Supreme Court, which ruled that men were better qualified than women, and then to the U.S. Supreme Court on grounds that the Idaho state law was unconstitutional. The Court agreed that it was. Chief Justice Burger writes that under the Equal Protection Clause, the basis of automatically preferring one class of people over another instead of evaluating individual qualifications must be reasonable, and that it is not reasonable to arbitrarily give preference to one sex over the other.*

*Warren Burger was the chief justice of the U.S. Supreme Court from 1969 to 1986. Previously he had been a judge of the U.S. Court of Appeals for the District of Columbia.*

Warren Burger, unanimous opinion, *Reed v. Reed*, U.S. Supreme Court, November 22, 1971.

Having examined the record and considered the briefs and oral arguments of the parties, we have concluded that the arbitrary preference established in favor of males by ... the Idaho Code cannot stand in the face of the Fourteenth Amendment's command that no State deny the equal protection of the laws to any person within its jurisdiction.

Idaho does not, of course, deny letters of administration to women altogether. Indeed, under [its law], a woman whose spouse dies intestate [without a will] has a preference over a son, father, brother, or any other male relative of the decedent. Moreover, we can judicially notice that in this country, presumably due to the greater longevity of women, a large proportion of estates, both intestate and under wills of decedents, are administered by surviving widows.

[The Idaho law] is restricted in its operation to those situations where competing applications for letters of administration have been filed by both male and female members of the same entitlement class established by [that law]. In such situations, [it] provides that different treatment be accorded to the applicants on the basis of their sex; it thus establishes a classification subject to scrutiny under the Equal Protection Clause.

## Classification of Persons Must Be Reasonable, Not Arbitrary

In applying that clause, this Court has consistently recognized that the Fourteenth Amendment does not deny to States the power to treat different classes of persons in different ways. The Equal Protection Clause of that amendment does, however, deny to States the power to legislate that different treatment be accorded to persons placed by a statute into different classes on the basis of criteria wholly unrelated to the objective of that statute. A classification "must be reasonable, not arbitrary, and must rest upon some ground of difference having a fair and substantial relation to the object of the legislation, so that all persons similarly circumstanced shall be

*Supporters of the Equal Rights Amendment carry a banner down Pennsylvania Avenue during a march in Washington, D.C., on the Friday, August 26, 1977.* AP Images.

treated alike" [*F.S. Royster Guano Co. v. Virginia*, 1920]. The question presented by this case, then, is whether a difference in the sex of competing applicants for letters of administration bears a rational relationship to a state objective that is sought to be advanced by the operation of [Idaho law].

In upholding the latter section, the Idaho Supreme Court concluded that its objective was to eliminate one area of controversy when two or more persons, equally entitled under [the law], seek letters of administration and thereby present the probate court "with the issue of which one should be named." The court also concluded that where such persons are not of the same sex, the elimination of females from consideration "is neither an illogical nor arbitrary method devised by the legislature to resolve an issue that would otherwise require a hearing as to the relative merits . . . of the two or more petitioning relatives. . . ."

Clearly the objective of reducing the workload on probate courts by eliminating one class of contests is not without some legitimacy. The crucial question, however, is whether [the Idaho law] advances that objective in a manner consistent with the command of the Equal Protection Clause. We hold that it does not. To give a mandatory preference to members of either sex over members of the other, merely to accomplish the elimination of hearings on the merits, is to make the very kind of arbitrary legislative choice forbidden by the Equal Protection Clause of the Fourteenth Amendment; and whatever may be said as to the positive values of avoiding intrafamily controversy, the choice in this context may not lawfully be mandated solely on the basis of sex.

# Children of Illegal Immigrants Are Entitled to Free Schooling

*William J. Brennan*

*The following selection is the majority opinion written by Supreme Court Justice William J. Brennan in the 1982 case of* Plyler v. Doe. *The controversial case was decided 5–4, with several of the justices writing concurring opinions and all four who disagreed joining the dissent. This ruling struck down a Texas law that denied state funds for educating the children of illegal immigrants. (James Plyler was a school superintendent, and "Doe" was the name used to represent the plaintiffs in a class action suit on the behalf of these children.) Speaking for the majority, Justice Brennan argues that the Equal Protection Clause of the Constitution's Fourteenth Amendment applies to everyone within a state, even people who entered the country illegally, and that it prohibits discriminating among them. Whereas illegal immigrants have committed a crime and are subject to deportation, their children are innocent of any wrongdoing and are entitled to the same benefits as other children. Furthermore, he says, education is more than a mere benefit; it is essential to the well-being of society. Not only will the children suffer lifelong effects if they are not educated, but the existence of a illiterate class would add to the state's cost for unemployment, welfare, and crime.*

*William J. Brennan, formerly a judge on the New Jersey Supreme Court, was a justice of the U.S. Supreme Court from 1956 to 1990. He was one of the Court's most influential liberal members.*

The Fourteenth Amendment provides that "[n]o State shall . . . deprive any person of life, liberty, or property, without due process of law; nor deny to any person within its jurisdic-

William J. Brennan, majority opinion, *Plyler v. Doe*, U.S. Supreme Court, June 15, 1982.

tion the equal protection of the laws." Appellants argue at the outset that undocumented aliens, because of their immigration status, are not "persons within the jurisdiction" of the State of Texas, and that they therefore have no right to the equal protection of Texas law. We reject this argument. Whatever his status under the immigration laws, an alien is surely a "person" in any ordinary sense of that term. Aliens, even aliens whose presence in this country is unlawful, have long been recognized as "persons" guaranteed due process of law by the Fifth and Fourteenth Amendments. Indeed, we have clearly held that the Fifth Amendment protects aliens whose presence in this country is unlawful from invidious discrimination by the Federal Government.

Appellants seek to distinguish our prior cases, emphasizing that the Equal Protection Clause directs a State to afford its protection to persons within its jurisdiction while the Due Process Clauses of the Fifth and Fourteenth Amendments contain no such assertedly limiting phrase. In appellants' view, persons who have entered the United States illegally are not "within the jurisdiction" of a State even if they are present within a State's boundaries and subject to its laws. Neither our cases nor the logic of the Fourteenth Amendment supports that constricting construction of the phrase "within its jurisdiction." We have never suggested that the class of persons who might avail themselves of the equal protection guarantee is less than coextensive with that entitled to due process. To the contrary, we have recognized that both provisions were fashioned to protect an identical class of persons, and to reach every exercise of state authority.

"The Fourteenth Amendment to the Constitution is not confined to the protection of citizens. It says: 'Nor shall any state deprive any person of life, liberty, or property without due process of law; nor deny to any person within its jurisdiction the equal protection of the laws.' These provisions are universal in their application, to all persons within the territorial jurisdiction, without regard to any differences of race, of color, or of nationality; and the protection of the laws is a pledge of the protection of equal laws." [*Yick Wo v. Hopkins*, 1886]

In concluding that "all persons within the territory of the United States," including aliens unlawfully present, may invoke the Fifth and Sixth Amendments to challenge actions of the Federal Government, we reasoned from the understanding that the Fourteenth Amendment was designed to afford its protection to all within the boundaries of a State. Our cases applying the Equal Protection Clause reflect the same territorial theme. . . .

## The Equal Protection Clause Applies to Everyone

There is simply no support for appellants' suggestion that "due process" is somehow of greater stature than "equal protection" and therefore available to a larger class of persons. To the contrary, each aspect of the Fourteenth Amendment reflects an elementary limitation on state power. To permit a State to employ the phrase "within its jurisdiction" in order to identify subclasses of persons whom it would define as beyond its jurisdiction, thereby relieving itself of the obligation to assure that its laws are designed and applied equally to those persons, would undermine the principal purpose for which the Equal Protection Clause was incorporated in the Fourteenth Amendment. The Equal Protection Clause was intended to work nothing less than the abolition of all caste-based and invidious class-based legislation. That objective is fundamentally at odds with the power the State asserts here to classify persons subject to its laws as nonetheless excepted from its protection. . . .

Use of the phrase "within its jurisdiction" thus does not detract from, but rather confirms, the understanding that the protection of the Fourteenth Amendment extends to anyone,

*A young girl holds a sign that reads "Indefinite Detention is Unconstitutional." She was one of many protesting indefinite detention of people by the Immigration and Naturalization Service before a federal courthouse in Seattle, Washington. AP Images.*

citizen or stranger, who is subject to the laws of a State, and reaches into every corner of a State's territory. That a person's initial entry into a State, or into the United States, was unlawful, and that he may for that reason be expelled, cannot negate the simple fact of his presence within the State's territorial perimeter. Given such presence, he is subject to the full range of obligations imposed by the State's civil and criminal laws. And until he leaves the jurisdiction—either voluntarily, or involuntarily in accordance with the Constitution and laws of the United States—he is entitled to the equal protection of the laws that a State may choose to establish. . . .

The Equal Protection Clause directs that "all persons similarly circumstanced shall be treated alike" [*F.S. Royster Guano Co. v. Virginia,* 1920]. But so too, "[t]he Constitution does not require things which are different in fact or opinion to be treated in law as though they were the same" [*Tigner v. Texas,* 1940]. . . . A legislature must have substantial latitude to establish classifications that roughly approximate the nature of the problem perceived, that accommodate competing concerns both public and private, and that account for limitations on the practical ability of the State to remedy every ill. In applying the Equal Protection Clause to most forms of state action, we thus seek only the assurance that the classification at issue bears some fair relationship to a legitimate public purpose.

But we would not be faithful to our obligations under the Fourteenth Amendment if we applied so deferential a standard to every classification. The Equal Protection Clause was intended as a restriction on state legislative action inconsistent with elemental constitutional premises. . . . It is appropriate to enforce the mandate of equal protection by requiring the State to demonstrate that its classification has been precisely tailored to serve a compelling governmental interest. . . .

Persuasive arguments support the view that a State may withhold its beneficence from those whose very presence within the United States is the product of their own unlawful conduct. These arguments do not apply with the same force to classifications imposing disabilities on the minor children of such illegal entrants. At the least, those who elect to enter our territory by stealth and in violation of our law should be prepared to bear the consequences, including, but not limited to, deportation. But the children of those illegal entrants are not comparably situated. . . .

## Public Education Is Important to Society

Public education is not a "right" granted to individuals by the Constitution. But neither is it merely some governmental "benefit" indistinguishable from other forms of social welfare legislation. Both the importance of education in maintaining our basic institutions, and the lasting impact of its deprivation on the life of the child, mark the distinction. . . .

In sum, education has a fundamental role in maintaining the fabric of our society. We cannot ignore the significant social costs borne by our Nation when select groups are denied the means to absorb the values and skills upon which our social order rests.

In addition to the pivotal role of education in sustaining our political and cultural heritage, denial of education to some isolated group of children poses an affront to one of the goals of the Equal Protection Clause: the abolition of governmental barriers presenting unreasonable obstacles to advancement on the basis of individual merit. Paradoxically, by depriving the children of any disfavored group of an education, we foreclose the means by which that group might raise the level of esteem in which it is held by the majority. But more directly, "education prepares individuals to be self-reliant and self-sufficient participants in society" [*Wisconsin v. Yoder*, 1972]. Illiteracy is an enduring disability. The inability to read and write will handicap the individual deprived of a basic education each and every day of his life. The inestimable toll of that deprivation on the social, economic, intellectual, and psychological well-being of the individual, and the obstacle it poses to individual achievement, make it most difficult to reconcile the cost or the principle of a status-based denial of basic education with the framework of equality embodied in the Equal Protection Clause. What we said 28 years ago in *Brown v. Board of Education*, still holds true:

> "Today, education is perhaps the most important function of state and local governments. . . . Today it is a principal instrument in awakening the child to cultural values, in preparing him for later professional training, and in helping him to adjust normally to his environment. In these days, it is doubtful that any child may reasonably be expected to succeed in life if he is denied the opportunity of an education. Such an opportunity, where the state has undertaken to provide it, is a right which must be made available to all on equal terms.". . .

[The Texas law] imposes a lifetime hardship on a discrete class of children not accountable for their disabling status. The stigma of illiteracy will mark them for the rest of their lives. By denying these children a basic education, we deny them the ability to live within the structure of our civic institutions, and foreclose any realistic possibility that they will contribute in even the smallest way to the progress of our Nation. In determining the rationality of [the law], we may appropriately take into account its costs to the Nation and to the innocent children who are its victims. In light of these countervailing costs, the discrimination contained in [that law] can hardly be considered rational unless it furthers some substantial goal of the State.

It is the State's principal argument, and apparently the view of the dissenting Justices, that the undocumented status of these children vel non ["or not"] establishes a sufficient rational basis for denying them benefits that a State might choose to afford other residents. . . . Faced with an equal protection challenge respecting the treatment of aliens, we agree that the courts must be attentive to congressional policy; the exercise of congressional power might well affect the State's prerogatives to afford differential treatment to a particular class of aliens. But we are unable to find in the congressional immigration scheme any statement of policy that might weigh significantly in arriving at an equal protection balance concerning the State's authority to deprive these children of an education. . . .

Appellants suggest that undocumented children are appropriately singled out because their unlawful presence within the United States renders them less likely than other children to remain within the boundaries of the State, and to put their education to productive social or political use within the State. Even assuming that such an interest is legitimate, it is an interest that is most difficult to quantify. The State has no assurance that any child, citizen or not, will employ the education provided by the State within the confines of the State's borders. In any event, the record is clear that many of the undocumented children disabled by this classification will remain in this country indefinitely, and that some will become lawful residents or citizens of the United States. It is difficult to understand precisely what the State hopes to achieve by promoting the creation and perpetuation of a subclass of illiterates within our boundaries, surely adding to the problems and costs of unemployment, welfare, and crime. It is thus clear that whatever savings might be achieved by denying these children an education, they are wholly insubstantial in light of the costs involved to these children, the State, and the Nation.

If the State is to deny a discrete group of innocent children the free public education that it offers to other children residing within its borders, that denial must be justified by a showing that it furthers some substantial state interest. No such showing was made here. Accordingly, the judgment of the Court of Appeals in each of these cases is affirmed.

# Congress, Not the Courts, Is Responsible for Policies Regarding Illegal Immigrants

*Warren Burger*

*In the following dissenting opinion in* Plyler v. Doe, *Supreme Court Chief Justice Warren Burger, joined by three other justices, argues that the Equal Protection Clause of the Fourteenth Amendment does not preclude the state from classifying people in order to determine their eligibility for government benefits, so long as the classification is not arbitrary or irrational, is not based on prejudice, and serves a legitimate government purpose. The fact that the children of illegal immigrants are innocent has no bearing on whether they are legally entitled to education, he says, because there are many government programs for which some people are ineligible even though they have done nothing wrong. There is no fundamental right to free education, and it is not irrational to reserve limited state funds for the benefit of lawful residents. Though Chief Justice Burger agrees that it is unwise to deny education to the children of illegal immigrants, he maintains that it is not unconstitutional. In his view it is a matter to be decided not by the courts but by the legislative branch.*

*Warren Burger was the chief justice of the U.S. Supreme Court from 1969 to 1986. Earlier, he had been a judge of the U.S. Court of Appeals for the District of Columbia. He was a conservative jurist who believed in a strict interpretation of the Constitution and disapproved of attempts by courts to take over functions belonging to the legislative branch of government.*

Were it our business to set the Nation's social policy, I would agree without hesitation that it is senseless for an enlightened society to deprive any children—including ille-

Warren Burger, dissenting opinion, *Plyler v. Doe*, U.S. Supreme Court, June 15. 1982.

gal aliens—of an elementary education. I fully agree that it would be folly—and wrong—to tolerate creation of a segment of society made up of illiterate persons, many having a limited or no command of our language. However, the Constitution does not constitute us as "Platonic Guardians" nor does it vest in this Court the authority to strike down laws because they do not meet our standards of desirable social policy, "wisdom," or "common sense." We trespass on the assigned function of the political branches under our structure of limited and separated powers when we assume a policymaking role as the Court does today. . . .

The Court's holding today manifests the justly criticized judicial tendency to attempt speedy and wholesale formulation of "remedies" for the failures—or simply the laggard pace—of the political processes of our system of government. The Court employs, and in my view abuses, the Fourteenth Amendment in an effort to become an omnipotent and omniscient problem solver. That the motives for doing so are noble and compassionate does not alter the fact that the Court distorts our constitutional function to make amends for the defaults of others. . . .

I have no quarrel with the conclusion that the Equal Protection Clause of the Fourteenth Amendment applies to aliens who, after their illegal entry into this country, are indeed physically "within the jurisdiction" of a state. However, as the Court concedes, this "only begins the inquiry." The Equal Protection Clause does not mandate identical treatment of different categories of persons.

The dispositive issue in these cases, simply put, is whether, for purposes of allocating its finite resources, a state has a legitimate reason to differentiate between persons who are lawfully within the state and those who are unlawfully there. The distinction the State of Texas has drawn—based not only upon its own legitimate interests but on classifications established by the Federal Government in its immigration laws and policies—is not unconstitutional.

## The Equal Protection Clause Does Not Prohibit Classifications Unless They Are Arbitrary

The Court acknowledges that, except in those cases when state classifications disadvantage a "suspect class" or impinge upon a "fundamental right," the Equal Protection Clause permits a state "substantial latitude" in distinguishing between different groups of persons. Moreover, the Court expressly—and correctly—rejects any suggestion that illegal aliens are a suspect class, or that education is a fundamental right. Yet by patching together bits and pieces of what might be termed quasi-suspect-class and quasi-fundamental-rights analysis, the Court spins out a theory custom-tailored to the facts of these cases.

In the end, we are told little more than that the level of scrutiny employed to strike down the Texas law applies only when illegal alien children are deprived of a public education. If ever a court was guilty of an unabashedly result-oriented approach, this case is a prime example.

The Court first suggests that these illegal alien children, although not a suspect class, are entitled to special solicitude under the Equal Protection Clause because they lack "control" over or "responsibility" for their unlawful entry into this country. Similarly, the Court appears to take the position that [the law] is presumptively "irrational" because it has the effect of imposing "penalties" on "innocent" children. However, the Equal Protection Clause does not preclude legislators from classifying among persons on the basis of factors and characteristics over which individuals may be said to lack "control." Indeed, in some circumstances persons generally, and children in particular, may have little control over or responsibility for such things as their ill health, need for public assistance, or place of residence. . . . The Equal Protection Clause protects against arbitrary and irrational classifications, and against invidious discrimination stemming from prejudice and hostility; it is not an all-encompassing "equalizer" designed to eradicate every distinction for which persons are not "responsible.". . .

The importance of education is beyond dispute. Yet we have held repeatedly that the importance of a governmental service does not elevate it to the status of a "fundamental right" for purposes of equal protection analysis. . . . Moreover, the Court points to no meaningful way to distinguish between education and other governmental benefits in this context. Is the Court suggesting that education is more "fundamental" than food, shelter, or medical care? . . .

The central question in these cases, as in every equal protection case not involving truly fundamental rights "explicitly or implicitly guaranteed by the Constitution" [*San Antonio Independent School District v. Rodriguez*, 1973], is whether there is some legitimate basis for a legislative distinction between different classes of persons. The fact that the distinction is drawn in legislation affecting access to public education—as opposed to legislation allocating other important governmental benefits, such as public assistance, health care, or housing—cannot make a difference in the level of scrutiny applied. . . .

## It Is Not Irrational to Save State Funds for Lawful Residents

The significant question here is whether the requirement of tuition from illegal aliens who attend the public schools—as well as from residents of other states, for example—is a rational and reasonable means of furthering the State's legitimate fiscal ends.

Without laboring what will undoubtedly seem obvious to many, it simply is not "irrational" for a state to conclude that it does not have the same responsibility to provide benefits for persons whose very presence in the state and this country is illegal as it does to provide for persons lawfully present. By definition, illegal aliens have no right whatever to be here, and the state may reasonably, and constitutionally, elect not to provide them with governmental services at the expense of those who are lawfully in the state. . . .

It is significant that the Federal Government has seen fit to exclude illegal aliens from numerous social welfare programs, such as the food stamp program, the old-age assistance, aid to families with dependent children, aid to the blind, aid to the permanently and totally disabled, and supplemental security income programs, the Medicare hospital insurance benefits program, and the Medicaid hospital insurance benefits for the aged and disabled program. Although these exclusions do not conclusively demonstrate the constitutionality of the State's use of the same classification for comparable purposes, at the very least they tend to support the rationality of excluding illegal alien residents of a state from such programs so as to preserve the state's finite revenues for the benefit of lawful residents. . . .

Denying a free education to illegal alien children is not a choice I would make were I a legislator. Apart from compassionate considerations, the long-range costs of excluding any children from the public schools may well outweigh the costs of educating them. But that is not the issue; the fact that there are sound policy arguments against the Texas Legislature's choice does not render that choice an unconstitutional one.

The Constitution does not provide a cure for every social ill, nor does it vest judges with a mandate to try to remedy every social problem. Moreover, when this Court rushes in to remedy what it perceives to be the failings of the political processes, it deprives those processes of an opportunity to function. When the political institutions are not forced to exercise constitutionally allocated powers and responsibilities, those powers, like muscles not used, tend to atrophy. Today's cases, I regret to say, present yet another example of unwarranted judicial action which in the long run tends to contribute to the weakening of our political processes.

# Laws That Discriminate on the Basis of Sexual Orientation Are Unconstitutional

*Anthony M. Kennedy*

Romer v. Evans *was a controversial 1996 Supreme Court case involving an amendment to the Colorado state constitution that invalidated local laws prohibiting discrimination against homosexuals. Supporters of this amendment, which was adopted through a statewide referendum, believed that it merely prevented the passage of laws giving special rights to gays—rights that many other citizens do not have. Opponents felt that it deprived gays of protection against injustices that other citizens do not encounter. The Court sided with the opponents, ruling that Colorado's constitutional amendment violated the Equal Protection Clause of the U.S. Constitution's Fourteenth Amendment. In his majority opinion, Justice Anthony M. Kennedy argues that the Colorado amendment seems to be based on nothing more than prejudice against a particular group of people, that it bears no relationship to any legitimate governmental purpose, and that there is no legal precedent for it. "It is a classification of persons undertaken for its own sake," Kennedy writes, "something the Equal Protection Clause does not permit."*

*Anthony M. Kennedy, who is not related to the Kennedy family prominent in American politics, has been a justice of the U.S. Supreme Court since 1988. He has often been the "swing vote" in 5–4 decisions in which the conservative and liberal members of the Court disagree.*

One century ago, the first Justice [John Marshall] Harlan admonished this Court that the Constitution "neither knows nor tolerates classes among citizens" [*Plessy v. Ferguson*,

Anthony M. Kennedy, majority opinion, *Romer v. Evans*, U.S. Supreme Court, May 20, 1996.

dissenting opinion]. Unheeded then, those words now are understood to state a commitment to the law's neutrality where the rights of persons are at stake. The Equal Protection Clause enforces this principle and today requires us to hold invalid a provision of Colorado's Constitution.

The enactment challenged in this case is an amendment to the Constitution of the State of Colorado, adopted in a 1992 statewide referendum. The parties and the state courts refer to it as "Amendment 2," its designation when submitted to the voters. The impetus for the amendment and the contentious campaign that preceded its adoption came in large part from ordinances that had been passed in various Colorado municipalities. . . . Amendment 2 repeals these ordinances to the extent they prohibit discrimination on the basis of "homosexual, lesbian or bisexual orientation, conduct, practices or relationships."

Yet Amendment 2, in explicit terms, does more than repeal or rescind these provisions. It prohibits all legislative, executive or judicial action at any level of state or local government designed to protect the named class, a class we shall refer to as homosexual persons or gays and lesbians. . . .

The State's principal argument in defense of Amendment 2 is that it puts gays and lesbians in the same position as all other persons. So, the State says, the measure does no more than deny homosexuals special rights. This reading of the amendment's language is implausible. . . .

## The Colorado Law Nullifies All Legal Protection for Gays

Amendment 2 bars homosexuals from securing protection against the injuries that . . . public-accommodations laws address. That in itself is a severe consequence, but there is more. Amendment 2, in addition, nullifies specific legal protections for this targeted class in all transactions in housing, sale of real estate, insurance, health and welfare services, private education, and employment.

## States Banning Discrimination Based on Sexual Orientation

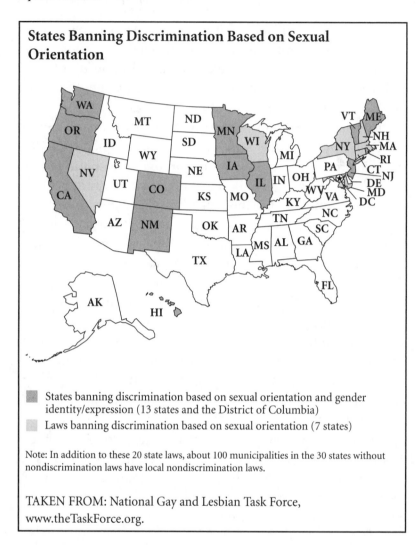

States banning discrimination based on sexual orientation and gender identity/expression (13 states and the District of Columbia)

Laws banning discrimination based on sexual orientation (7 states)

Note: In addition to these 20 state laws, about 100 municipalities in the 30 states without nondiscrimination laws have local nondiscrimination laws.

TAKEN FROM: National Gay and Lesbian Task Force, www.theTaskForce.org.

Not confined to the private sphere, Amendment 2 also operates to repeal and forbid all laws or policies providing specific protection for gays or lesbians from discrimination by every level of Colorado government. . . .

Amendment 2's reach may not be limited to specific laws passed for the benefit of gays and lesbians. It is a fair, if not necessary, inference from the broad language of the amendment that it deprives gays and lesbians even of the protection of general laws and policies that prohibit arbitrary discrimination in governmental and private settings. . . .

We cannot accept the view that Amendment 2's prohibition on specific legal protections does no more than deprive homosexuals of special rights. To the contrary, the amendment imposes a special disability upon those persons alone. Homosexuals are forbidden the safeguards that others enjoy or may seek without constraint. They can obtain specific protection against discrimination only by enlisting the citizenry of Colorado to amend the state constitution or perhaps, on the state's view, by trying to pass helpful laws of general applicability. This is so no matter how local or discrete the harm, no matter how public and widespread the injury. We find nothing special in the protections Amendment 2 withholds. These are protections taken for granted by most people either because they already have them or do not need them; these are protections against exclusion from an almost limitless number of transactions and endeavors that constitute ordinary civic life in a free society.

## The Colorado Law Bears No Rational Relationship to Legitimate State Interests

The Fourteenth Amendment's promise that no person shall be denied the equal protection of the laws must co-exist with the practical necessity that most legislation classifies for one purpose or another, with resulting disadvantage to various groups or persons. We have attempted to reconcile the principle with the reality by stating that, if a law neither burdens a fundamental right nor targets a suspect class, we will uphold the legislative classification so long as it bears a rational relation to some legitimate end.

Amendment 2 fails, indeed defies, even this conventional inquiry. First, the amendment has the peculiar property of imposing a broad and undifferentiated disability on a single named group, an exceptional and, as we shall explain, invalid form of legislation. Second, its sheer breadth is so discontinuous with the reasons offered for it that the amendment seems inexplicable by anything but animus [ill will] toward the class that it affects; it lacks a rational relationship to legitimate state interests. . . .

In the ordinary case, a law will be sustained if it can be said to advance a legitimate government interest, even if the law seems unwise or works to the disadvantage of a particular group, or if the rationale for it seems tenuous. The laws challenged in [this Court's previous cases] were narrow enough in scope and grounded in a sufficient factual context for us to ascertain that there existed some relation between the classification and the purpose it served. By requiring that the classification bear a rational relationship to an independent and legitimate legislative end, we ensure that classifications are not drawn for the purpose of disadvantaging the group burdened by the law.

Amendment 2 confounds this normal process of judicial review. It is at once too narrow and too broad. It identifies persons by a single trait and then denies them protection across the board. The resulting disqualification of a class of persons from the right to seek specific protection from the law is unprecedented in our jurisprudence. The absence of precedent for Amendment 2 is itself instructive; "[d]iscriminations of an unusual character especially suggest careful consideration to determine whether they are obnoxious to the constitutional provision" [*Louisville Gas & Elec. Co. v. Coleman*, 1928].

It is not within our constitutional tradition to enact laws of this sort. Central both to the idea of the rule of law and to our own Constitution's guarantee of equal protection is the principle that government and each of its parts remain open on impartial terms to all who seek its assistance. "'Equal protection of the laws is not achieved through indiscriminate imposition of inequalities'" [*Sweatt v. Painter*, 1950]. Respect for this principle explains why laws singling out a certain class of citizens for disfavored legal status or general hardships are rare. A law declaring that in general it shall be more difficult for one group of citizens than for all others to seek aid from the government is itself a denial of equal protection of the laws in the most literal sense. . . .

A second and related point is that laws of the kind now before us raise the inevitable inference that the disadvantage imposed is born of animosity toward the class of persons affected. "[I]f the constitutional conception of 'equal protection of the laws' means anything, it must at the very least mean that a bare . . . desire to harm a politically unpopular group cannot constitute a legitimate governmental interest" [*Department of Agriculture v. Moreno*, 1973]. Even laws enacted for broad and ambitious purposes often can be explained by reference to legitimate public policies which justify the incidental disadvantages they impose on certain persons. Amendment 2, however, in making a general announcement that gays and lesbians shall not have any particular protections from the law, inflicts on them immediate, continuing, and real injuries that outrun and belie any legitimate justifications that may be claimed for it. We conclude that, in addition to the far-reaching deficiencies of Amendment 2 that we have noted, the principles it offends, in another sense, are conventional and venerable; a law must bear a rational relationship to a legitimate governmental purpose, and Amendment 2 does not.

The primary rationale the State offers for Amendment 2 is respect for other citizens' freedom of association, and in particular the liberties of landlords or employers who have personal or religious objections to homosexuality. Colorado also cites its interest in conserving resources to fight discrimination against other groups. The breadth of the Amendment is so far removed from these particular justifications that we find it impossible to credit them. We cannot say that Amendment 2 is directed to any identifiable legitimate purpose or discrete objective. It is a status-based enactment divorced from any factual context from which we could discern a relationship to legitimate state interests; it is a classification of persons undertaken for its own sake, something the Equal Protection Clause does not permit. . . .

We must conclude that Amendment 2 classifies homosexuals not to further a proper legislative end but to make them unequal to everyone else. This Colorado cannot do. A State cannot so deem a class of persons a stranger to its laws. Amendment 2 violates the Equal Protection Clause, and the judgment of the Supreme Court of Colorado is affirmed.

# The Constitution Does Not Require Preferential Treatment for Gays

*Antonin Scalia*

*In his dissenting opinion in* Romer v. Evans, *Supreme Court Justice Antonin Scalia states that contrary to the Court's assertion, the amendment to Colorado's state constitution would not deprive gays of any legal rights that other citizens have, but only of special rights based on their sexual orientation. He argues that because laws against homosexual conduct are considered constitutional (this was true at the time this case was decided, although such laws have since been struck down), it cannot be unconstitutional to pass laws against giving favored treatment to homosexuals. Furthermore, he says, there is precedent for laws that attempt to preserve majority views of sexual morality—for example, the constitutions of some states subject polygamists to much more severe treatment than denial of favored status. The Court's ruling in this case suggests to Justice Scalia that those provisions are unconstitutional unless polygamists have fewer constitutional rights than homosexuals. "The people of Colorado," he writes, "have adopted an entirely reasonable provision which does not even disfavor homosexuals in any substantive sense, but merely denies them preferential treatment."*

*Antonin Scalia has been a justice of the Supreme Court since 1986. He is a strong conservative who holds an "originalist" view of the Constitution, which means that he believes in interpreting the Constitution as it was understood at the time of its adoption rather than on the basis of modern conditions.*

Antonin Scalia, dissenting opinion, *Romer v. Evans*, U.S. Supreme Court, May 20, 1996.

The Court has mistaken a Kulturkampf [a conflict between cultures] for a fit of spite. The constitutional amendment before us here is not the manifestation of a "'bare . . . desire to harm'" homosexuals, but is rather a modest attempt by seemingly tolerant Coloradans to preserve traditional sexual mores against the efforts of a politically powerful minority to revise those mores through use of the laws. That objective, and the means chosen to achieve it, are not only unimpeachable under any constitutional doctrine hitherto pronounced (hence the opinion's heavy reliance upon principles of righteousness rather than judicial holdings); they have been specifically approved by the Congress of the United States and by this Court.

In holding that homosexuality cannot be singled out for disfavorable treatment, the Court contradicts a decision, unchallenged here, pronounced only 10 years ago, and places the prestige of this institution behind the proposition that opposition to homosexuality is as reprehensible as racial or religious bias. Whether it is or not is precisely the cultural debate that gave rise to the Colorado constitutional amendment (and to the preferential laws against which the amendment was directed). Since the Constitution of the United States says nothing about this subject, it is left to be resolved by normal democratic means, including the democratic adoption of provisions in state constitutions. This Court has no business imposing upon all Americans the resolution favored by the elite class from which the Members of this institution are selected, pronouncing that "animosity" toward homosexuality is evil. I vigorously dissent. . . .

## The Colorado Law Merely Prohibits Special Treatment for Gays

[The Colorado Court's] analysis, which is fully in accord with (indeed, follows inescapably from) the text of the constitutional provision, lays to rest such horribles, raised in the course of oral argument, as the prospect that assaults upon homo-

*Justice Antonin Scalia was appointed to the United State Supreme Court in 1986.* Supreme Court of the United States.

sexuals could not be prosecuted. The amendment prohibits special treatment of homosexuals, and nothing more. It would not affect, for example, a requirement of state law that pensions be paid to all retiring state employees with a certain length of service; homosexual employees, as well as others, would be entitled to that benefit. But it would prevent the

State or any municipality from making death-benefit payments to the "life partner" of a homosexual when it does not make such payments to the long-time roommate of a nonhomosexual employee. Or again, it does not affect the requirement of the State's general insurance laws that customers be afforded coverage without discrimination unrelated to anticipated risk. Thus, homosexuals could not be denied coverage, or charged a greater premium, with respect to auto collision insurance; but neither the State nor any municipality could require that distinctive health insurance risks associated with homosexuality (if there are any) be ignored.

Despite all of its hand-wringing about the potential effect of Amendment 2 on general antidiscrimination laws, the Court's opinion ultimately does not dispute all this, but assumes it to be true. The only denial of equal treatment it contends homosexuals have suffered is this: They may not obtain preferential treatment without amending the state constitution. That is to say, the principle underlying the Court's opinion is that one who is accorded equal treatment under the laws, but cannot as readily as others obtain preferential treatment under the laws, has been denied equal protection of the laws. If merely stating this alleged "equal protection" violation does not suffice to refute it, our constitutional jurisprudence has achieved terminal silliness.

The central thesis of the Court's reasoning is that any group is denied equal protection when, to obtain advantage (or, presumably, to avoid disadvantage), it must have recourse to a more general and hence more difficult level of political decisionmaking than others. The world has never heard of such a principle, which is why the Court's opinion is so long on emotive utterance and so short on relevant legal citation. And it seems to me most unlikely that any multilevel democracy can function under such a principle. For whenever a disadvantage is imposed, or conferral of a benefit is prohibited, at one of the higher levels of democratic decisionmaking (i.e., by the state legislature rather than local government, or by the people at large in the state constitution rather than the legislature), the affected group has (under this theory) been denied equal protection. To take the simplest of examples, consider a state law prohibiting the award of municipal contracts to relatives of mayors or city councilmen. Once such a law is passed, the group composed of such relatives must, in order to get the benefit of city contracts, persuade the state legislature—unlike all other citizens, who need only persuade the municipality. It is ridiculous to consider this a denial of equal protection, which is why the Court's theory is unheard-of. . . .

## The Colorado Law Has a Rational Basis

I turn next to whether there was a legitimate rational basis for the substance of the constitutional amendment—for the prohibition of special protection for homosexuals. It is unsurprising that the Court avoids discussion of this question, since the answer is so obviously yes. The case most relevant to the issue before us today is not even mentioned in the Court's opinion: In *Bowers v. Hardwick* [1986], we held that the Constitution does not prohibit what virtually all States had done from the founding of the Republic until very recent years—making homosexual conduct a crime. That holding is unassailable, except by those who think that the Constitution changes to suit current fashions. But in any event it is a given in the present case: Respondents' briefs did not urge overruling *Bowers*, and at oral argument respondents' counsel expressly disavowed any intent to seek such overruling. If it is constitutionally permissible for a State to make homosexual conduct criminal, surely it is constitutionally permissible for a State to enact other laws merely disfavoring homosexual conduct. . . . And a fortiori [even more] it is constitutionally permissible for a State to adopt a provision not even disfavoring homosexual conduct, but merely prohibiting all levels of state government from bestowing special protections upon homosexual conduct. . . .

No principle set forth in the Constitution, nor even any imagined by this Court in the past 200 years, prohibits what Colorado has done here. But the case for Colorado is much stronger than that. What it has done is not only unprohibited, but eminently reasonable, with close, congressionally approved precedent in earlier constitutional practice.

First, as to its eminent reasonableness. The Court's opinion contains grim, disapproving hints that Coloradans have been guilty of "animus" or "animosity" toward homosexuality, as though that has been established as Unamerican. Of course it is our moral heritage that one should not hate any human being or class of human beings. But I had thought that one could consider certain conduct reprehensible—murder, for example, or polygamy, or cruelty to animals—and could exhibit even "animus" toward such conduct. Surely that is the only sort of "animus" at issue here: moral disapproval of homosexual conduct, the same sort of moral disapproval that produced the centuries-old criminal laws that we held constitutional in *Bowers*. The Colorado amendment does not, to speak entirely precisely, prohibit giving favored status to people who are homosexuals; they can be favored for many reasons—for example, because they are senior citizens or members of racial minorities. But it prohibits giving them favored status because of their homosexual conduct—that is, it prohibits favored status for homosexuality.

But though Coloradans are, as I say, entitled to be hostile toward homosexual conduct, the fact is that the degree of hostility reflected by Amendment 2 is the smallest conceivable. The Court's portrayal of Coloradans as a society fallen victim to pointless, hate-filled "gay-bashing" is so false as to be comical. . . .

By the time Coloradans were asked to vote on Amendment 2. . . . the Governor of Colorado had signed an executive order pronouncing that "in the state of Colorado we recognize the diversity in our pluralistic society and strive to bring an end to discrimination in any form," and directing state agency-heads to "ensure non-discrimination" in hiring and promotion based on, among other things, "sexual orientation." I do not mean to be critical of these legislative successes; homosexuals are as entitled to use the legal system for reinforcement of their moral sentiments as are the rest of society. But they are subject to being countered by lawful, democratic countermeasures as well.

That is where Amendment 2 came in. It sought to counter both the geographic concentration and the disproportionate political power of homosexuals by (1) resolving the controversy at the statewide level, and (2) making the election a single-issue contest for both sides. It put directly, to all the citizens of the State, the question: Should homosexuality be given special protection? They answered no. The Court today asserts that this most democratic of procedures is unconstitutional. Lacking any cases to establish that facially absurd proposition, it simply asserts that it must be unconstitutional, because it has never happened before. . . .

## If Homosexuals Are Given Favored Status, Why Not Polygamists?

But there is a much closer analogy, one that involves precisely the effort by the majority of citizens to preserve its view of sexual morality statewide, against the efforts of a geographically concentrated and politically powerful minority to undermine it. The constitutions of the States of Arizona, Idaho, New Mexico, Oklahoma, and Utah to this day contain provisions stating that polygamy is "forever prohibited." Polygamists, and those who have a polygamous "orientation," have been "singled out" by these provisions for much more severe treatment than merely denial of favored status; and that treatment can only be changed by achieving amendment of the state constitutions. The Court's disposition today suggests that these provisions are unconstitutional, and that polygamy must be permitted in these States on a state-legislated, or perhaps even local-option, basis—unless, of course, polygamists for some reason have fewer constitutional rights than homosexuals.

The United States Congress, by the way, required the inclusion of these antipolygamy provisions in the constitutions of Arizona, New Mexico, Oklahoma and Utah, as a condition of their admission to statehood. . . . Thus, this "singling out" of the sexual practices of a single group for statewide, democratic vote—so utterly alien to our constitutional system, the Court would have us believe—has not only happened, but has received the explicit approval of the United States Congress. . . .

I think it no business of the courts (as opposed to the political branches) to take sides in this culture war. But the Court today has done so, not only by inventing a novel and extravagant constitutional doctrine to take the victory away from traditional forces, but even by verbally disparaging as bigotry adherence to traditional attitudes. To suggest, for example, that this constitutional amendment springs from nothing more than "'a bare . . . desire to harm a politically unpopular group'" [quoting from *Department of Agriculture v. Moreno*, 1973], is nothing short of insulting. (It is also nothing short of preposterous to call "politically unpopular" a group which enjoys enormous influence in American media and politics, and which, as the trial court here noted, though composing no more than 4% of the population had the support of 46% of the voters on Amendment 2). . . .

Today's opinion has no foundation in American constitutional law, and barely pretends to. The people of Colorado have adopted an entirely reasonable provision which does not even disfavor homosexuals in any substantive sense, but merely denies them preferential treatment. Amendment 2 is designed to prevent piecemeal deterioration of the sexual morality favored by a majority of Coloradans, and is not only an appropriate means to that legitimate end, but a means that Americans have employed before. Striking it down is an act, not of judicial judgment, but of political will. I dissent.

# The Supreme Court's Rulings on Equal Protection Have Been Inconsistent

*Geoffrey R. Stone*

*In the following selection, based on a speech given to the Federal Bar Association, University of Chicago professor Geoffrey R. Stone explains the reasoning behind the U.S. Supreme Court's decision in* Bush v. Gore, *which determined the outcome of the 2000 presidential election. The Court held that the method of recounting ballots in Florida was inconsistent and therefore violated the Equal Protection Clause of the Constitution's Fourteenth Amendment. Although this ruling was widely criticized, in Stone's opinion there was some basis for it. However, he says, under federal law the outcome of a contested election should be decided by Congress, not by the Supreme Court. Furthermore, he suggests that the personal political views of some of the justices influenced the decision, because three of those who voted for it had, in past cases, usually voted against protection under the Fourteenth Amendment for disadvantaged blacks, women, gays, and the poor.*

*Geoffrey R. Stone is the Harry L. Kalven Jr. Distinguished Service Professor of Law at the University of Chicago. He is the coeditor of the* Supreme Court Review.

In *Bush v. Gore*, candidate [George W.] Bush challenged the December 8, 2000 decision of the Florida Supreme Court on two constitutional grounds. He argued that the decision of the Florida Supreme Court allowing a recount of disputed ballots [cast in the presidential election] violated both Article II, Section 1 and the Equal Protection Clause of the Fourteenth Amendment of the US Constitution. . . .

Geoffrey R. Stone, "Equal Protection? The Supreme Court's Decision in *Bush v. Gore*," University of Chicago: Fathom Digital Collection, 2004. Reproduced by permission. http://fathom.lib.uchicago.edu/1/777777122240.

Let me turn now to the real heart of the case—the Supreme Court's holding that the decision of the Florida Supreme Court violated the Equal Protection Clause of the Fourteenth Amendment. The crux of this holding is captured in the majority's observation that, although the "intent of the voter" standard "is unobjectionable as an abstract proposition," a constitutional problem nonetheless "inheres in the absence of specific standards to ensure its equal application."

The majority were concerned that, in searching for the "intent of the voter," and in giving meaning to ballots with dimpled and hanging chads, "the standards for accepting or rejecting contested ballots might vary not only from county to county but [even] within a single county." The majority therefore concluded that the "recount mechanisms implemented [by] the Florida Supreme Court do not satisfy the minimum requirement for non-arbitrary treatment of voters necessary to secure the fundamental right" to equal protection.

Although this argument was endorsed by seven of the nine Justices—all but [John Paul] Stevens and [Ruth Bader] Ginsburg—it has generally been treated with derision by liberal and conservative commentators alike. As my liberal colleague Cass Sunstein has noted, the Court's Equal Protection conclusion "lacked all support in precedent and history . . . and clearly ignored a host of problems as serious as those it addressed." Not to be outdone, my conservative colleague Richard Epstein has sniped that the Court's equal protection argument is "a confused nonstarter at best, which deserves much of the scorn that has been heaped upon it."

Frankly, I am more sympathetic to the Court's reasoning than most of its critics, but let me begin with the scorn. What do the critics say? First, they point out that this argument is entirely unprecedented and, indeed, comes completely out of the blue. This is essentially true.

Beginning in 1964, in decisions like *Harper v. Virginia Board of Elections*, which invalidated the poll tax, and *Reynolds v. Sims,* which invalidated malapportioned legislative districts, the Warren Court [i.e., the Supreme Court under Chief Justice Earl Warren] first embraced the principle that laws that grant the right to vote on a selective basis must be carefully scrutinized because they affect the very "foundation of our representative government."

Although the question posed in *Bush v. Gore* was quite different from the ones posed in cases like *Harper* and *Reynolds,* which involved laws that clearly discriminated against readily identifiable groups of voters, the principle underlying those early Warren Court decisions could, in my judgment, support the Court's conclusion in *Bush v. Gore* that, in counting votes, a State must use standards and processes that ensure that ballots are counted in a consistent and equal manner.

However, and here's the rub, it's been some thirty years since the Supreme Court of the United States has actually applied the principles articulated in cases like *Harper* and *Reynolds,* and both the [Warren] Burger and [William H.] Rehnquist Courts, and most of the Justices who eagerly embraced this argument in *Bush v. Gore,* have steadfastly rejected this principle for the better part of three decades. . . .

## The Scope of the Decision Was Limited

Second, critics of the Court's Equal Protection analysis in *Bush* have noted the rather peculiar limitations the majority attempted to place on the implications of their own logic. For example, in a curious effort to constrain the reach of their decision, the majority pointedly noted that "our consideration" of the Equal Protection Clause's impact on election processes "is limited to the present circumstances."

Moreover, and more to the point, the majority explicitly declared that "the question before the Court is not whether local entities . . . may develop different systems for implementing elections" within a single State. In other words, although holding that the use of the "intent of the voter" standard to count ballots violates the Equal Protection Clause because that standard can be applied differently in different parts of a State, the majority expressly eschewed saying anything about the much more dramatic Equal Protection problem presented by the Florida election process—the fact that different counties and precincts used very different voting technologies, that those different technologies had very different probabilities of undercounting the votes of individual citizens, and that there was a clear correlation between the use of those technologies that maximized undercounting and the relative poverty of the citizens of a particular county or precinct.

As Professor Pam Karlan of the Stanford Law School has observed: "A court that believes that the real problem in Florida was the disparities in the manual recount standards, rather than the disparities in a voter's overall chance of casting a ballot that is actually counted, has strained at a gnat only to ignore an elephant."

Now, in fairness to the majority, I think there may be at least a partial answer to this criticism. It is a long-standing principle of First Amendment law that the standardless licensing of speech is unconstitutional. A city, for example, may not constitutionally grant a governmental official standardless authority to decide which speakers can and cannot speak in a city park. Rather, to limit the risk of discriminatory application, the city must expressly focus the licensing official's authority on such permissible considerations as time, place and manner, and must expressly prohibit the official's consideration of such impermissible factors as the content of the speech.

One might argue, by analogy, that in counting votes in an election, a State must define with similar clarity the specific factors that may be considered in deciding whether a particular ballot is or is not to be counted, and that the "intent of the voter" standard is simply too vague to be relied upon in the highly charged context of vote-counting. Thus, in order to limit the possible abuse of discretion, the State arguably must specify precisely whether it will or will not count dimpled or hanging chads as "legal votes.". . .

## There Was No Crisis Demanding Speed

Third, the majority's five-to-four decision not to remand the case to enable Florida to conduct a constitutionally appropriate recount with a more specific definition of "intent of the voter" has been attacked by almost everyone. The majority asserted that because the Florida legislature may have intended to take advantage of the "safe harbor" provision of federal law, which required a selection of electors by December 12—the date of the Supreme Court's decision, there was simply no time left for any further recount.

There is virtually no one who will defend this conclusion as a matter of law. . . .

How, then, can one explain the refusal of these five Justices to remand the case to Florida for a further recount consistent with their interpretation of the Equal Protection Clause? Some of the Court's most fervent apologists have argued that these Justices, in a burst of noble pragmatism, did the nation a service by putting an end to a controversy that was threatening to spin out of control. Frankly, I would have been more impressed with these particular Justices' nobility if the consequence of their decision had been to install as president the Democratic candidate for the job.

But, in the actual circumstances presented, I find this argument wishful, at best. There was, in fact, no political crisis facing the nation. There was no social unrest, no paralysis of government, no lack of discipline in foreign affairs, no instability in the financial markets, no crisis in consumer confidence, no stockpiling of goods. Perhaps there was too much

C-SPAN, but that hardly threatens the Republic. Surely, there was no more of a crisis facing the nation during the Bush/Gore post-election dispute than there was during the abortive attempt to impeach the President. But no one called that to a halt to avoid a "crisis."

Would a further recount have been messy? You bet. There were all sorts of things that could have gone wrong after December 12 both in Florida and in Congress, and not many that could have gone right. But was this a constitutionally legitimate reason for the Supreme Court of the United States to halt the recount of legal votes in Florida? No.

The plain and simple fact is that if this matter could not have been finally resolved in Florida prior to the convening of the Electoral College, the appropriate forum for determining the outcome of the presidential election was Congress, the politically accountable branch of government and the branch that is expressly charged both by the Constitution and by federal law with this responsibility. No one has given this authority to the Supreme Court of the United States. . . .

In *Bush v. Gore*, the five-member majority ignored . . . the law itself. Their decision to prevent Florida from counting what the Court itself accepted as "legal votes" under state law may have been pragmatic, but it was not lawful.

## Politics in Black Robes?

I'd like to conclude with what, for me, is the most dispiriting facet of this whole sorry episode. I had the great privilege of serving as a law clerk to a Justice of the United States Supreme Court. For more than a decade, I have edited the *Supreme Court Review* and I co-author the nation's leading constitutional law casebook. I have taught constitutional law for more than a quarter of a century, even while serving as dean and provost.

As a teacher of constitutional law, I am frequently asked by skeptical students: Isn't constitutional law just politics in black robes? Don't the Justices just vote their political preferences? Isn't all this "stuff" about the Constitution merely a charade? I have always rejected this understanding of the Supreme Court and of constitutional law.

The cases presented to the Supreme Court are rarely governed by clear precedent. If the cases were easy, they would not be in the Supreme Court. Moreover, the Court is frequently called upon to give meaning to the highly opened-textured provisions of our Constitution: "Congress shall make no law abridging the freedom of speech." "No State shall deny to any person the equal protection of the laws." "No person shall be deprived of life, liberty or property without due process of law." These terms are not self-defining.

In this context, it is hardly surprising that individual Justices will often decide specific controversies in ways that reflect their personal backgrounds, experiences, values and institutional assumptions. In the absence of controlling precedent and self-defining language, it is inevitable that the Justices will bring such considerations to bear in giving meaning to the fundamental guarantees of our Constitution. How they think about equality, or liberty or federalism or poverty or efficiency will inescapably affect this understanding of these provisions.

This is both inevitable and appropriate, and it is as true for so-called liberal Justices as it is for the conservatives. But what has sustained my faith in the Supreme Court as an institution, and in constitutional law as a fundamental part of our legal and political system, is the fact that, regardless of their partisan affiliations, the Justices historically have strived sincerely and in good conscience to give fair meaning to the guarantees of our Constitution. They do not trade votes, or accept bribes, or allow partisan political considerations to dictate their decisions.

And that brings me back to *Bush v. Gore.*

The majority's decision in *Bush v. Gore* that the recount process ordered by the Florida Supreme Court violated the

Equal Protection Clause was a highly activist, but plausible interpretation of the Constitution. What was disheartening to me was not the constitutional principle embraced by the majority, but the votes cast by Justice [William H.] Rehnquist, [Antonin] Scalia and [Clarence] Thomas in support of that decision, votes that were dispositive of the case, and of the presidency of the United States.

No one familiar with the jurisprudence of Justices Rehnquist, Scalia and Thomas could possibly have imagined that they would vote to invalidate the Florida recount process on the basis of their own well-developed and oft-invoked approach to the Equal Protection Clause.

## Inconsistent Voting Record of Some Justices

In the decade leading up to *Bush v. Gore*, Justices Rehnquist, Scalia and Thomas cast approximately 65 votes in non-unanimous Supreme Court decisions interpreting the Equal Protection Clause. Nineteen of those votes were cast in cases involving affirmative action, and I will return to them in a moment. Of the 46 votes that these Justices cast in cases that did not involve affirmative action, Justices Rehnquist, Scalia and Thomas collectively cast only two votes to uphold a claimed violation of the Equal Protection Clause. Thus, these three Justices found a violation of Equal Protection in only 4 percent of these cases.

For the sake of comparison, over this same period, and in these very same cases, the colleagues of Justices Rehnquist, Scalia and Thomas collectively voted 74 percent of the time to uphold the Equal Protection Clause claim. 74 percent versus 4 percent.

Against this background, one must wonder why Justices Rehnquist, Scalia and Thomas suddenly discovered power and beauty in the Equal Protection Clause in *Bush v. Gore*. Indeed, as a group they cast more votes (three, to be exact) to uphold the Equal Protection Clause claim in *Bush v. Gore* than they had previously cast in all of the non-affirmative action Equal Protection Clause cases that they had considered in the previous decade.

Of course, those other cases were different, for they involved laws that disadvantaged blacks, women, gays, the disabled and the poor—groups that are surely less deserving of concern under the Equal Protection Clause than the beneficiary of the Court's decision in *Bush*.

But this is not a fair characterization. After all, I have excluded from the above analysis the votes of Justices Rehnquist, Scalia and Thomas in affirmative action cases. In those cases, these three Justices have consistently demonstrated the same spirit of bold and innovative interpretation of the Equal Protection Clause that they manifested in *Bush v. Gore*. Indeed, over the past decade, these three Justices have collectively cast 19 votes to hold unconstitutional various forms of affirmative action. This represents 100 percent of their votes in these cases—a perfect record. (Their colleagues, by contrast, have voted only 33 percent of the time to invalidate such programs.)

What does this tell us? It tells us that Justices Rehnquist, Scalia and Thomas have a rather distinctive view of the United States Constitution. Apparently the Equal Protection Clause, which was enacted after the Civil War primarily to protect the rights of newly freed slaves, is to be used for two and only two purposes—to invalidate affirmative action and to invalidate the recount process in the 2000 presidential election.

As Professor Robert Post of the Berkeley Law School has observed, "I do not know a single person who believes that if the parties were reversed, if Gore were challenging a recount ordered by a Republican Florida Supreme Court," that Justices Rehnquist, Scalia and Thomas "would have reached for a startling and innovative principle of constitutional law to hand Gore the victory."

You can draw your own conclusions.

CONSTITUTIONAL
AMENDMENTS
BEYOND THE BILL OF RIGHTS

CHAPTER 4

# Current Debate on Equal Protection

# Banning of Same-Sex Marriage Will Someday Be Ruled Unconstitutional

*Kermit Roosevelt*

*In the following viewpoint, published on the fortieth anniversary of the U.S. Supreme Court ruling that declared laws against interracial marriage unconstitutional under the Equal Protection Clause of the Fourteenth Amendment, Kermit Roosevelt offers his opinion as to why it took a hundred years after the adoption of the amendment for that to happen. The Equal Protection Clause does not prohibit all discrimination, he says, only discrimination that is intended to oppress a particular group or brand its members as inferior. If there is a rational justification for discrimination, it is not unconstitutional. In the past most people believed there was a rational justification for banning interracial marriage, but social attitudes changed, and now such bans seem obviously unjustifiable. The same thing, Roosevelt says, is happening with respect to homosexuality, and therefore prohibition of same-sex marriage is likely to be ruled unconstitutional in the future. He argues that this will not be the result of activism on the part of judges but will merely reflect a widespread shift in people's views.*

*Kermit Roosevelt is a professor at the University of Pennsylvania Law School and the author of* The Myth of Judicial Activism.

In June 1958, Virginia residents Richard Loving and Mildred Jeter traveled to the District [of Columbia], got married and returned home. An unexceptional story but for one fact:

Richard was white and Mildred black. Their marriage therefore violated Virginia's Racial Integrity Act. The Lovings were convicted in Virginia court and sentenced to a year in jail, with the sentence suspended on the condition that they leave Virginia and not return together for 25 years.

They got back sooner. On June 12, 1967—40 years ago next Tuesday—the Supreme Court struck down Virginia's ban on interracial marriages. Writing for a unanimous court, Chief Justice Earl Warren stated that the restriction served no purpose but that of "invidious racial discrimination" and therefore violated the equal protection clause of the 14th Amendment.

*Loving v. Virginia* is a constitutional icon now, not least because of its wonderful name. But its continued relevance might not be obvious. Nowadays everyone agrees that bans on interracial marriages are unconstitutional, and even if they weren't, few people would support them. But *Loving* illustrates something important about the evolution of constitutional law.

The place to start is simple. The equal protection clause was ratified in 1868, but it took a century for the court to prohibit laws banning interracial marriage. If the decision is so obviously right, why did it take so long?

One answer might be that the court was waiting for the proper political climate. *Brown v. Board of Education*, handed down in 1954, aroused tremendous resistance, and the court might reasonably have concluded that it should wait before pressing further.

## Supreme Court Decisions Reflect Shifts in Social Attitudes

But this answer is too simple. Yes, there would have been political resistance then, but it would have been based on the argument that the Constitution did not *require* states to allow interracial marriage. And at some earlier time this argument

*A gay couple exchange marriage vows before an Episcopalian priest.* AP Images.

would have been correct. The equal protection clause guarantees only "the equal protection of the laws." It does not explic-

itly prohibit all discrimination. The best the court has done over the years to define the prohibited kind is to say that the clause bars "invidious" discrimination—discrimination designed to oppress a particular group or to brand its members as inferior. If reasonable justifications for discrimination exist, it is constitutionally permissible.

Interracial marriage bans now seem obviously invidious. But go back far enough and the consensus flips. At one point, most everyone thought such bans were legitimate. The same is true of segregated schooling and discrimination against women. It is true of just about everything the Supreme Court has held that the equal protection clause prohibits: At one point, all of these practices were seen as legitimate reflections of the world, not as invidious attempts to impose inequality. When the court held these practices unconstitutional, it was neither enforcing a rule that had existed since 1868 nor creating a new rule. It was recognizing that social attitudes had shifted, and with them the understanding about what is reasonable and what is invidious.

This point connects *Loving* to current social struggles, most notably the debate over same-sex marriage. Opponents decry the "activist judges" in Massachusetts who struck down that state's same-sex marriage ban and warn that the Supreme Court will someday follow. So it may—but, if it does, responsibility will not lie primarily with judges.

The past few decades have brought a dramatic change in social attitudes about homosexuality. The American Psychiatric Association, which once classified homosexuality as a mental disease, abandoned that position in 1973. Public opinion polls show an increasing acceptance of homosexuality, and state legislatures are beginning to follow. Restricting the benefits of marriage to opposite-sex couples is increasingly seen as invidious, an inequality inflicted for no good reason.

If the trend continues, this view eventually will find expression at the Supreme Court level, just as it did in *Loving*. This is not judicial activism. It is how we make the Constitution ours.

# A Constitutional Amendment Should Be Adopted to Ban Same-Sex Marriage

*Richard Land*

*In the following viewpoint Richard Land comments on an Iowa judge's ruling that a state law allowing marriage only between a man and a woman violates the constitutional rights of due process and equal protection, arguing that such rulings threaten the view of marriage held by the majority of voters. Same-sex marriage is a national rather than a state issue, he says, and eventually there will be one definition of marriage throughout the nation. In Land's opinion, most people are opposed to same-sex marriage and would support a constitutional amendment banning it. He expresses the belief that this should be made an issue in the next presidential election.*

*Richard Land is the president of the Southern Baptist Ethics & Religious Liberty Commission and the host of the nationally syndicated radio program* For Faith and Family.

A county judge in Des Moines, Iowa, of all places, ruled last month that the state law allowing marriage only between a man and a woman violates the constitutional rights of due process and equal protection.

This isn't New York or Massachusetts or California, mind you—this is our nation's heartland.

Iowa voters, with their own defense of marriage act in place for over a decade, thought they had settled the issue of same-sex marriage. While the judge's decision has now been stayed, this action reminds us that the institution of marriage is still under constant threat from the whims of just one obscure judge.

Richard Land, "A Constitutional Tipping Point on Marriage," *For Faith and Family*, September 12, 2007. Reproduced by permission. http://faithandfamily.com/article/a-constitutional-tipping-point-on-marriage.

Anyone paying attention to the early-developing race for the White House knows that Iowa—with its first-in-the-nation presidential caucus—is crawling with aspirants for the Oval Office. Perhaps this decision by an Iowa judge will help place this issue front-and-center in the minds of voters across the nation and thus, the presidential candidates.

While some opponents of same-sex marriage argue that this is a state issue, I believe at its heart it is a national issue. In fact, I believe events in American history support this position.

I suspect that Abraham Lincoln was a staunch Federalist. While he believed most issues should be decided at the state level, there are some issues that are so compelling and basic ("first principles") that they have to be decided at the federal level. Lincoln understood the moral dilemma that would unfold if each state was able to decide for itself whether it would be "slave" or "free."

In a speech delivered June 17, 1858—before he became president—Lincoln said the issue of slavery was a "crisis" that the nation could not ignore.

Quoting the Bible, he said, "A house divided against itself cannot stand" (Matt. 12:25).

"I believe this government cannot endure permanently half slave and half free," Lincoln continued. "I do not expect the Union to be dissolved; I do not expect the house to fall; but I do expect it will cease to be divided. It will become all one thing, or all the other. Either the opponents of slavery will arrest the further spread of it, and place it where the public mind shall rest in the belief that it is in the course of ultimate extinction, or its advocates will push it forward till it shall become alike lawful in all the States, old as well as new, North as well as South."

I have ancestors who fought for the Confederacy, as well as ancestors who fought for the Union, and I appreciate the fact that the Civil War was more complicated than just the issue of slavery. There are people who assert the war was about states' rights and not about slavery. What do you think was the precipitating cause that made people talk about states' rights? It was some people's belief that it was a state's right to allow some people to own other people. The fact is, without the issue of slavery, there never would have been a Civil War.

## There Must Be One Definition of Marriage Throughout the Nation

The slavery analogy is apt when it comes to the marriage issue. America's families—and the culture at large—cannot survive as a union of states with half embracing same-sex marriage and half accepting only traditional marriage. The U.S. government will not disintegrate, but eventually the nation will have one definition of marriage binding us all.

Lincoln gave his speech in the same year that the infamous Dred Scott decision was decided by the Supreme Court. The sensibilities of many Americans of that day were outraged by this immoral decision that said, for the purposes of law, that slaves were not people, but property.

The Dred Scott decision was not what you would call a close decision. The 7–2 verdict said the right to own slaves was a fundamentally guaranteed constitutional right that could not be limited by the states.

Lincoln, in an 1860 address, pointed out that the slaveholders would not be content to continue owning slaves in the states where they held them. They wanted to force everyone in the country to acknowledge their right to have slaves anywhere in the United States. In other words, they wanted to make slavery legal in every state of the union.

So less than six months after the end of the Civil War, what did the people of the United States do? They adopted the Thirteenth Amendment to the Constitution, which said once and for all that "neither slavery nor involuntary servitude, except as a punishment for crime, whereof the party

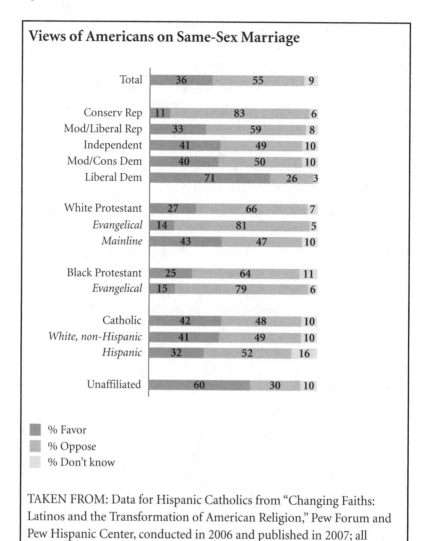

## Views of Americans on Same-Sex Marriage

| | % Favor | % Oppose | % Don't know |
|---|---|---|---|
| Total | 36 | 55 | 9 |
| Conserv Rep | 11 | 83 | 6 |
| Mod/Liberal Rep | 33 | 59 | 8 |
| Independent | 41 | 49 | 10 |
| Mod/Cons Dem | 40 | 50 | 10 |
| Liberal Dem | 71 | 26 | 3 |
| White Protestant | 27 | 66 | 7 |
| *Evangelical* | 14 | 81 | 5 |
| *Mainline* | 43 | 47 | 10 |
| Black Protestant | 25 | 64 | 11 |
| *Evangelical* | 15 | 79 | 6 |
| Catholic | 42 | 48 | 10 |
| *White, non-Hispanic* | 41 | 49 | 10 |
| *Hispanic* | 32 | 52 | 16 |
| Unaffiliated | 60 | 30 | 10 |

■ % Favor
■ % Oppose
■ % Don't know

TAKEN FROM: Data for Hispanic Catholics from "Changing Faiths: Latinos and the Transformation of American Religion," Pew Forum and Pew Hispanic Center, conducted in 2006 and published in 2007; all other data from Pew Research Center survey, 2007.

shall have been duly convicted, shall exist within the United States or any place subject to their jurisdiction."

Slavery was outlawed in the federal Constitution. It was not going to be an issue decided by each state.

I respect the Constitution, and I don't believe it should be amended unless it is absolutely necessary. We have reached the point regarding marriage that we once reached regarding slavery. Rulings like this one in Iowa reveal the urgent need for a federal Marriage Protection Amendment.

At least one person has said to me that while banning slavery expanded personal liberty, prohibiting same-sex marriage would contract or limit personal liberty. Yet while the ban on slavery expanded liberty for the slaves, it inhibited and constricted liberty for the slaveholders.

In fact, the emancipation of the 3 million African-Americans held in involuntary servitude until the end of the Civil War was the largest property expropriation without any kind of indemnity or compensation to the slaveholders that has taken place anywhere in the Western world in modern history.

No longer was an American free to own another human being. Liberty was secured for the slaves and constricted for slaveholders. Never has justice been better served.

Forbidding same-sex couples from marrying may be a constriction of their liberty, but more importantly, *it is an expansion of the people's liberty to define what constitutes marriage.*

Whether or not the same-sex marriage issue becomes a topic of discussion among those running for president depends upon all of us. If we make the definition of marriage as between a man and a woman an issue, it will become an issue among the crowd of candidates reaching for the golden ring.

# The Federal Hate Crimes Bill Would Violate the Concept of Equal Protection

*Robert H. Knight*

*In the following viewpoint Robert H. Knight argues that the federal hate crimes legislation being reviewed by the Senate at the time he was writing would violate the principle of equal protection under the law. All crime victims deserve equal protection, he points out, but under the proposed law, crimes motivated by hate would be prosecuted and punished more severely than others. This, Knight says, would amount to punishing thoughts, which is a system common in totalitarian regimes, whereas "in a free society, our system concerns itself with actions, not beliefs." The law that Knight discusses was not passed. A similar bill was introduced in 2007, but as of August 2008, it remained stalled in Congress.*

*Robert H. Knight is the director of the Culture & Family Institute, an affiliate of the organization Concerned Women for America.*

The hate crimes bill, an amendment to the Child Safety Act (H.R. 3132), was passed by the U.S. House of Representatives on September 15 [2005]. Titled "The Local Law Enforcement Enhancement Act," the bill is [as of 2005] under review in the U.S. Senate. This bill:

- Lays the groundwork for a severe threat to religious freedom.

Robert H. Knight, "The Federal Hate Crimes Bill: Federalizing Criminal Law While Threatening Civil Liberties," *Concerned Women for America*, September 29, 2005. Reproduced by permission. www.cwfa.org/articledisplay.asp?id=9069&department= CFI&categoryid=papers.

- Expands federal power enormously into cases tradition-ally handled by the states.

- Creates "thought crime," which has no place in Ameri-can law.

- Violates the concept of equal protection under the law.

- Tempts law enforcement agencies into giving some crime victims' cases more priority than others.

- Brings hate crime politics into the schools.

- Is unnecessary, given 1) there is no evidence that such cases are not receiving proper prosecution and sentenc-ing, and that 2) hate crimes have been decreasing over the past three years, not increasing.

During the Supreme Court hearings in 2000 on the Boy Scout case [*Boy Scouts of America v. Dale*, in which the Court considered whether the Boy Scouts' ban on gay leaders was unconstitutional], pro-life Rev. Rob Schenck was sitting in the audience next to the Clinton White House liaison for "gay" is-sues. Thinking the pastor was a fellow liberal, the woman whispered, "We're not going to win this case, but that's okay. Once we get 'hate crime' laws on the books, we're going to go after the Scouts and all the other bigots."

## Threat to Religious Freedom

Similar hate crime laws are already being used in Canada, Sweden and elsewhere to persecute and prosecute Christians and others who hold traditional beliefs regarding homosexual-ity.

It's already happening in the United States as well. Under Pennsylvania's newly enacted "hate crimes" law, 11 Christians ware arrested and jailed overnight in 2004 for singing and preaching in a Philadelphia public park at a homosexual street festival. Five of them, including a 17-year-old girl, were bound

*A pastor holds signs protesting homosexuality outside the Albany County Courthouse, where one of the defendants in the beating murder of Matthew Shepard stood trial in 1999. AP Images.*

over and charged with five felonies and three misdemeanors. After several months, during which the defendants faced possible 47-year prison sentences, a judge finally dismissed the charges. But she also noted that unpopular speech such as that expressed by Nazis and the Ku Klux Klan are protected. In other words, the court upheld the free speech right of the Christians, but placed their speech in the same category as that of odious hate groups.

Homosexual activists have redefined any opposition to homosexuality as "hate speech." Laws already criminalize speech that incites violence. It's easy to imagine a scenario in which any incident involving a homosexual can be blamed on people who have publicly opposed homosexual activism.

## Expanding Federal Power

Under Section 607 2-B, the bill authorizes federal intervention under several circumstances, including a crime that:

1. interferes with commercial or other economic activity in which the victim is engaged at the time of the conduct; or

2. otherwise affects interstate or foreign commerce.

Under Section 607 (b) (2) (D), the bill allows federal intervention if:

> "The verdict or sentence obtained pursuant to State charges left demonstratively unvindicated the Federal interest in eradicating bias-motivated violence."

"One can hardly imagine a more vague or broad invitation for federal prosecutors than 'unvindicated' and 'federal interest,'" said Jan LaRue, Concerned Women for America's (CWA's) chief counsel. "This gives the U.S. Attorney General the discretion to enter any case he or she wants, and will politicize criminal prosecution. Special interests will lobby to have their cases treated more seriously than other crime victims' and local authorities will be hapless to object."

The language in the House version of the hate crimes bill adds not only "sexual orientation" to a list of newly protected classes, but "gender identity." Final passage would mean that the Congress of the United States would be officially creating a new civil rights category based on sexual confusion. Like "sexual orientation," "gender identity" is infinitely flexible, and includes transvestitism (cross-dressing) and transsexualism (believing that one is in the wrong sex's body and sometimes surgically changing one's sex organs).

## Creating "Thought Crime"

In a free society, our system concerns itself with actions, not beliefs.

CWA's LaRue explains:

"The prosecutor must prove both a guilty act and a guilty mind in order to convict a person of a crime. A guilty mind is proved by the intent to commit the prohibited act, such as pointing a loaded gun at the victim and pulling the trigger. Intent is not the same as motive. Motive has to do with why the defendant wanted to shoot the victim. Motive is not an element of the crime. When it can be proved by the evidence, it is icing on the cake for the prosecution. Motive is highly subjective, and in the case of a hate crime, it is in the eyes of the prosecutor who can use evidence unrelated to the crime to prove the motive.

"To understand the difference and the unfairness to different victims, imagine that A is convicted of intentionally shooting B and is sentenced to 10 years in prison. Nothing about A's motive was mentioned whatsoever. Now imagine that A is convicted of intentionally shooting C. The prosecutor proves that A did it and he did it because of something critical A said or wrote about homosexual conduct, which has nothing to do with C, yet it is used to prove A was motivated by 'bias' against C because C is a homosexual. A is sentenced to 10 years plus the enhanced sentence provided under the hate crime law. If you were B, what message would the difference in sentencing send to you about the value of your life?" LaRue asks.

By adding sentencing enhancement for some crimes, based on the motive or perceptions of the offender, the United States would move toward a system found commonly in totalitarian regimes, which punish thoughts or beliefs not sanctioned by the government. In effect, a suspect is convicted not only of the crime but also convicted of the crime of having a particular belief.

## Violating Equal Protection

All crime victims deserve equal protection under the law. Hate crime laws, however, create a multi-tiered system of justice, in which some crime victims' cases are taken more seriously than others. Often, such cases are media-driven, as occurred in Wyoming in 1999 during the trial of two men accused of the 1998 murder of college student Matthew Shepard.

By contrast, the case of Kristin Lamb, an 8-year-old Wyoming girl killed and thrown into a landfill about a month before Mr. Shepard's murder, received no publicity, indicating that her life was not worth as much as Mr. Shepard's. The court in Wyoming, which had no "hate crimes" law on the books, gave Shepard's two murderers the maximum penalty. A Wyoming official testified during U.S. Senate hearings that because of the media frenzy, his office spent a budget-crushing amount on the case, including for media management.

## Tempting Local Officials

Under Section 604, the hate crimes bill creates a program that would dispense federal grants of up to $100,000 to state and local officials for criminal investigations and prosecution of hate crimes.

This is an incentive for departments to place more emphasis on politically driven cases at the expense of others. Seeking federal dollars, police and prosecutors will define more and more cases as "hate crimes." Expect such crimes to soar. After California enacted a "hate crimes" law, incidents went from 75 to 2,052 in four years.

## Enlisting Schools
## in Pro-Gay Campaigns

Under Section 604 (2), the Office of Justice Programs is empowered to ensure compliance with "the local infrastructure developed under the grants." Affected parties include "community groups and schools, colleges, and universities."

Schools are already incorporating pro-homosexual materials in sex education and "anti-bullying" programs sponsored by private groups such as the Gay, Lesbian and Straight Education Network (GLSEN) and Parents, Family and Friends of Lesbians and Gays (PFLAG). These programs inform schoolchildren that homosexual behavior is normal and healthy, and that people (and religions) that oppose it are hate-filled bigots. The hate crimes bill amounts to a Christmas tree for taxpayer-assisted propaganda programs that advance acceptance of homosexuality in the schools while denigrating people of faith.

## An Unnecessary Addition

There is no evidence that hate crime cases are being mishandled by local and state authorities. Proponents have yet to provide data to show that federal intervention is needed to ensure justice.

What's more, according to the last three annual FBI Crime in the United States Uniform Crime Reports, hate crimes are decreasing, including those based on "sexual orientation."

The hate crimes bill undermines equal protection; is a direct threat to freedom; would federalize criminal law, and would transform the nature of criminal law by criminalizing thoughts and beliefs instead of actions.

We [the CWA] have multiple objections to the bill, but our first concern is this: Any senator or representative who votes for such a bill is helping to erect a system in which our children will be jailed someday for their beliefs.

# Hate Crime Laws Are Necessary Because Not All Citizens Are Yet Equal

*Mel Seesholtz*

*In the following viewpoint Mel Seesholtz argues that although hate crime laws appear to violate the Equal Protection Clause of the Fourteenth Amendment by treating some instances of the same crime differently than others, they are needed because gays are not yet treated equally. He suggests that a hate crime is really two crimes: the criminal act itself and the threat that it poses to other members of the class against which it is committed. Some Christians have used scare tactics to oppose hate crime laws, claiming, for instance, they would interfere with freedom of speech—but, Seesholtz points out, that is not true because such laws apply only to acts of violence. Opponents of homosexuality would still be free to speak against it even if it were added to the classes protected under those laws. Fortunately, he says, other Christians are speaking out against those who misuse religious teachings to disguise prejudice and discrimination. But in his opinion, until all citizens are actually equal under the law, hate crime laws will be necessary.*

*Mel Seesholtz is a professor in the English Department at Pennsylvania State University.*

At first glance, hate-crime laws may seem unnecessary. Section 1 of the Fourteenth Amendment to the U.S. Constitution reads:

"All persons born or naturalized in the United States, and subject to the jurisdiction thereof, are citizens of the United

Mel Seesholtz, "Hate-Crime Laws Should Not Be Necessary, But . . . ," *Atlantic Free Press*, May 7, 2007. Reproduced by permission of the author. www.atlanticfreepress.com/content/view/1518/81/.

States and of the State wherein they reside. No State shall make or enforce any law which shall abridge the privileges or immunities of citizens of the United States; nor shall any State deprive any person of life, liberty, or property, without due process of law; nor deny to any person within its jurisdiction the equal protection of the laws."

"Equal protection" should mean equal protection afforded to equal citizens. Hate-crime laws seem to make crimes against some citizens worse than the same crimes committed against other citizens. After the House passed H.R. 1952 [a federal hate crimes bill introduced in 2007], Tony Perkins of the Family Research Council argued that "the actions of a majority of the House today undermine the promise of equal protection under the law guaranteed by the 14th Amendment."

## A Hate Crime Is Two Crimes

But all citizens are not equal. Gay Americans cannot legally marry [each other] (except in Massachusetts), nor can they serve openly in the military. And in more than a few jurisdictions they can still be denied housing or employment because of their sexual orientation. Moreover, as Eric Zorn pointed out in a *Chicago Tribune* piece, a case can be made for a hate-crime being two crimes:

"The simplest answer to this is that when hatred for a particular group or class or race is the obvious motive for an attack, that attack becomes, in effect, two crimes. The first is the offense itself. The second is the implicit threat that offense makes to other members of that group, class or race."

"That second crime has new victims."

"Consider an incident in which someone uses spray paint to deface the garage of a house into which a gay family has just moved."

"The crime is vandalism, no matter what. But to argue against the idea of hate crimes is to argue that it shouldn't matter at all to the law whether the graffiti is a smiley face or some hostile, anti-gay slur."

"The smiley face is a petty annoyance. The hateful slogan is, in effect, a threat to other gay people in the area—they might be next."

"Is it fair to limit hate-crime protection to certain classes of people? My argument is yes, that historical and cultural contexts cause certain classes of people to feel legitimately threatened by hate-inspired crimes that do not really threaten other classes of people."

The current federal hate-crime law applies to violent crimes committed due to the victim's race, color, national origin, or religion. It's highly doubtful any of those currently "protected" by this law would advocate its repeal. It's highly likely they'd argue such "protection" is not only needed but deserved for reasons Mr. Zorn noted.

Then along came H.R. 1592, the Local Law Enforcement Hate Crimes Prevention Act of 2007. It added sexual orientation, gender, gender identity, and disability to the federal hate-crime law.

## Hatred Toward Gays Is Common

According to the FBI, every day twenty-five Americans are victims of hate crimes. One in six of those hate crimes is motivated by the victim's sexual orientation. As for what Mr. Zorn called "historical and cultural contexts," homosexuals have consistently been demeaned, denigrated and discriminated against.

During the McCarthy era more homosexuals were "weeded out" and fired than Communists. Gays were regularly barred from taverns and restaurants, barred from public assembly, barred from using the U.S. Postal Service to send newsletters.

In 1953 President Dwight Eisenhower signed an executive order barring homosexuals from government jobs as well as many from other forms of employment. Homosexuals had no freedom of assembly or speech and could be arrested on simple suspicion—behaviors such as "gesturing with limp wrists," walking "with a sway to the hips," and "wearing tight fitting trousers"—and sent to mental hospitals until "cured," despite claims by prison doctors that "cures" were not possible.

H.R. 1592—also known as the Matthew Shepard Act—had broad public and bipartisan support, including 73 percent of the American people and more than 210 law enforcement, civil rights, civic and religious organizations. Similar legislation had previously passed both houses of Congress, but was ultimately derailed by the then Republican leadership as they cowered to the dictates of religion-based lobby groups.

As soon as it was reintroduced into the current Congressional session, the rabidly anti-gay Christian Right once again flew into a tizzy. As the bill's passage became more and more certain, they launched a hysterical campaign against it. Apparently sacrificing the disabled was a small price to pay in order to keep gays excluded.

Aside from blatant lies—so unbecoming for "Christian" leaders—they also resorted to tactics such as distributing doctored Congressional testimony, a Jesus Christ "wanted poster," and promoting a video produced by a known white-supremacist—"John Smith"—whose other titles include *Keep America White* and *Black Intelligence.*

Dominionist leaders of the Christian Right—men like James Dobson of Focus on the Family, Louis Sheldon of Traditional Values Coalition, Don Wildmon of American Family Association, Tony Perkins of Family Research Council—screeched in unison that H.R. 1592 would put pastors at risk and target evangelicals if they preached against homosexuality and argued that gay Americans did not deserve equal civil rights. On 26 April 2007, Louis Sheldon, chairman of the Traditional Values Coalition—the "high minded" group that distributed the Jesus "wanted poster" and a comic titled "Congress Declares April Drag Queen Month"—sent out an action alert. The subject line read "Pastors Protect Yourself from Jail—Distribute this Alert."

The Christian Right's campaign was based *solely* on lies and deceitful scare tactics.

## The Law Would Not Affect Freedom of Speech

The title of the bill exposed that: "Hate *Crimes*." H.R. 1592, like the existing hate-crime law, would apply *only* to acts of violence *after* they'd been committed. Pulpit pastors and the self-righteous would still be able to exercise their freedom of speech and say things like "Homosexuality is sinful," "Homosexuality is an abomination to God" and yes, even invoke Westboro Baptist Church's mantras "God hates fags" and "Fags die, God laughs." That's their Constitutional right, just as others have the right to say the leaders of the Christian Right are malignant bigots who hide behind a twisted version of religion in order to promote discrimination and enhance their own political power.

The Christian Right claims homosexuality is nothing more than a choice—unlike race, color, and national origin—and those practicing the "lifestyle" should not, therefore, be protected. Their claim is based on no legitimate scientific or medical facts. Indeed, virtually all credible research points to homosexuality being outside the realm of choice.

But what is an indisputable fact is that one's religion is absolutely 100 percent a choice. Would Dobson, Sheldon, Wildmon, and Perkins support removing "religion" from the wording of the current federal hate-crime law?

In the days to come the Christian Right will, no doubt, be busy lobbying the Senate to kill H.R. 1592 and launching campaigns to bolster the president's will to veto the bill should it clear the Senate. The [George W.] Bush administration is, of course, encouraging and patronizing them with it announcement of a probable veto: "If H.R. 1592 were presented to the President, his senior advisors would recommend that he veto the bill."

Whatever the ultimate fate of H.R. 1592, it's already served a purpose. It's exposed—yet again—the leaders of the Christian Right and their organizations for what they are: liars and bigots hiding behind a bastardized form of "religion."

## Many Christians Oppose Discrimination Against Gays

Fortunately, true Christians are speaking up and acting:

> "The nondenominational group Faith in America today announced the launch of a five-city 'Call to Courage' campaign to educate Americans about what it calls the misuse of religious teachings to discriminate and isolate LGBT [lesbian, gay, bisexual, transgender] people. . . ."

> "'We're asking Americans to be courageous and to join us in a stand against discrimination in all forms. As a nation, we have exhibited such courage in the past by rejecting the use of religion to sanction slavery and the subjugation of women,' said Mitchell Gold, founder of Faith In America. . ."

> "This campaign is a first step toward putting an end to bigotry disguised as religious truth and creating a just world where everyone will be allowed to flourish in America without prejudice."

Faith in America is right. What's needed is for more fair-minded Americans to find the courage to stand up to bigots and those who use tainted religion to justify and promote discrimination for their own sinister political purposes. Until that happens, and until all Americans enjoy *equal* civil rights—

including the right to marry and serve in the military—the Fourteenth Amendment's promise of "equal protection" is hollow.

Hate-crime laws should not be needed, but for the time being, they are necessary.

# A Woman Is Entitled to Equal Protection When She Did Not Consent to Pregnancy

*Eileen McDonagh*

*In the following viewpoint Northeastern University professor Eileen McDonagh argues that because the Equal Protection Clause of the Fourteenth Amendment requires the state to treat similarly situated people in the same way, a woman should be as much entitled to defense against an unborn child as she would be to defense against any other use of her body to which she has not consented. Consent to sex does not necessarily mean consent to pregnancy, McDonagh says, and yet to prohibit abortion would give more rights to a fetus than to a born child—women are not forced to donate blood or organs to born children or anyone else. The government would protect a woman from other nonconsensual use of her body; therefore, in McDonagh's opinion, under the Equal Protection Clause it should assist women in self-defense against unwanted pregnancy.*

*Eileen McDonagh is a professor of political science at Northeastern University and the author of* Breaking the Abortion Deadlock: From Choice to Consent.

It is time for the pro-choice position to recast itself in a proactive, rather than a re-active, mode. Rather than merely holding on to what we have in *Roe* [*Roe v. Wade*, 1973], it is time to start building upon *Roe* to secure for women not only the right to choose an abortion, but also the right to public assistance for obtaining one.

To go on the offensive, pro-choice advocates must find a way to mandate state action to assist women in obtaining

Eileen McDonagh, "Adding Consent to Choice in the Abortion Debate," *Society*, July/August 2005. Reproduced by permission of the publisher and author. www.springer link.com/content/nuqat42j7d6v47cf/.

abortions, and, by extension, to retract policies that hinder women from obtaining them. The American Constitution does not mandate that the state must act, as cases such as *De-Shaney* have clearly established [*DeShaney v. Winnebago County*, 1989, in which the Supreme Court held that the state has no obligation to intervene in cases of domestic abuse]. However, the Equal Protections Clause of the Fourteenth Amendment does mandate that the state must treat similarly situated people in the same way, particularly when state action involves fundamental rights, such as the right to make reproductive choices. Thus, to mandate the state to act to assist women in obtaining an abortion requires reframing abortion rights using the Equal Protections Clause, rather than merely the Due Process Clause. This is a strategy that many constitutional law scholars have tried. However, they have not done so by using the third way to think about abortion rights: Pro-Consent.

The pro-consent approach to abortion rights redefines with whom a woman is similarly situated when she seeks an abortion. It does so by focusing on the medical and legal definitions of pregnancy as the "condition in a woman's body resulting from a fertilized ovum and later a fetus." Medically, even a "normal pregnancy" is a massive transformation of a woman's body, one that raises her blood pressure, and her heart rate, elevates her hormones to 1,000 times their base level, reroutes all of her blood to flow through the body of the fetus, and grows a new organ in her body, the placenta. Legally, if a woman does not consent to the massive transformation of her body resulting from the fetus, she is being injured by the fetus. Though it has no conscious intention to do so.

## Consent to Sex Does Not Require Consent to Pregnancy

A woman's consent to the act of sexual intercourse with a man does not require her to consent to the condition of pregnancy, any more than the right to consent to the act of sexual intercourse requires a person to consent to any other condition subsequent to that act, such as acquiring AIDS. The Pro-Consent Foundation for abortion rights is constitutionally powerful, because even if the fetus were granted the same rights as a born person, fetal rights would not include the right to transform, massively, a woman's physical body, since no born person has such a right. Once a child is born, for example, no state in the country requires a parent to give even a pint of blood to a child, much less bone marrow or organ transplants. To require a woman to give her blood, organs, and every cell of her body to the fetus grants the fetus *more* rights than a born child, not less. Even pro-life advocates don't ask for more rights for the fetus. What they are asking for are the same rights as a born child.

If anyone sought to take from a woman, without her consent, her blood, bone marrow, or in any other way invade her body to obtain resources necessary to sustain the life of another person, the government would step in to protect the woman from such a massive, non-consensual use of her body—this would hold, even if the intended recipient were the woman's own born child. Thus, to the degree that the government protects people from non-consensual use, intrusion, and transformation of their bodies by others, the government becomes obligated, on the basis of the Equal Protection Clause of the Fourteenth Amendment, to assist a woman in her self-defense against the massive use and transformation of her body resulting from the fetus. . . .

The [Supreme] Court has ruled that strict scrutiny must apply when evaluating the constitutionality of state policies that impinge upon fundamental rights, such as bodily integrity and liberty. State policies involving fundamental rights require the state to treat people who are similarly situated in a similar way. When a woman does not consent to pregnancy, the fetus situates her similarly to other victims of harm to their bodily integrity and liberty. To the degree that the state protects people from legal and medical harm to their bodily integrity and liberty, the Equal Protection Clause mandates that the state must protect a woman from the legal and/or medical harm of a nonconsensual pregnancy. State failure to do so deprives a woman of her constitutional right to equal protection and her fundamental right to bodily integrity and liberty. . . .

Even if the fetus were constructed to be a person, albeit a mentally incompetent one, the state would need to offer assistance to women against the harm resulting from a fetus, similar to the way the state assists other people who are victims of harm resulting from mentally incompetent people. State failure to do so—or state delay in doing so (e.g., being made to wait a 24-hour waiting period)—would deny to women equal protection of their bodily integrity and liberty.

## What the Fetus "Is" What the Fetus "Does"

Currently: What the fetus "is" determines abortion rights. The two major approaches to abortion rights, pro-life and pro-choice generally are seen as being the opposite of each other. Yet what is more striking is what they have in common: namely, both agree that abortion rights depend upon what the fetus "is," and, more specifically, both agree that if the fetus is a person, then a woman does not have a right to an abortion.

This premise is clear in pro-life language that depicts the fetus as a little citizen in the womb, who is "in charge of" the woman's pregnancy. Although a woman may choose what to do with her body, she has no right to make a choice (an abortion) that necessarily kills an innocent human being (the fetus). Thus, the pro-life position is that if the fetus is a person, then a woman does not have a right to an abortion. For this reason, pro-life activists spend enormous effort to prove that the fetus *is* a person, and, thus, that a woman does not have a right to an abortion.

Pro-choice activists accept the pro-life premise that if the fetus is a person, then a woman does not have a right to an abortion. Lead lawyer in *Roe*, Sarah Weddington, explicitly conceded this point in oral argument before the Court, and Justice [Harry A.] Blackmun referred to her concession in the *Roe* decision itself. The Court skirted the personhood issue of the fetus by refusing to take such a position in the face of so much disagreement among philosophers, physicians, and lawyers. Instead, the Court in *Roe* simply stated that even if the fetus is a person, because it is not a born person, it is not covered by Constitutional protections in general, or the Fourteenth Amendment in particular. . . .

The pro-consent argument for abortion rights is a prototypical "sameness" argument. It asserts that women, as well as men, have a right to bodily integrity and liberty that is so fundamental that it includes the right to self-defense against one's own offspring, whether that offspring is a fetus in the womb or a born child. Although the maternal thing to do would be to carry a pregnancy to term and find a supportive adoptive home for the born infant, women have not only maternal identities, but human identities as well. As such, following along the lines of this argument, women, as human beings, are morally, constitutionally, and politically justified in obtaining an abortion because the fetus has no more inherent right to use and massively transform a woman's body than does a born child. What is more, to the degree that the government assists other human beings in their self-defense against state-protected entities, the government is obligated to assist a woman in her self-defense against a fetus. If anything, since the entire police power of the state already clearly entails assisting people in their self-defense in relation to other people, defining the fetus as a person with the same rights as a born person strengthens, rather than weakens, a woman's right to government assistance in obtaining an abortion.

# An Unborn Child Is Entitled to Equal Protection Under the Fourteenth Amendment

*Charles I. Lugosi*

*In this viewpoint Charles I. Lugosi argues that unborn children are persons and therefore have a right to equal protection under the Fourteenth Amendment; the Supreme Court's failure to define them as such is merely a matter of judicial interpretation. If the Court were to do so, abortion would be illegal in all states. In Lugosi's opinion, it is immoral to exclude the unborn from the scope of the Equal Protection Clause. Furthermore, he says, it is not the role of the government to protect women from alleged violence within the womb because pregnancy is a natural condition.*

*Charles I. Lugosi is a Canadian attorney who has taught in the law schools of both American and Canadian universities.*

Since fetuses and embryos on an objective modern scientific basis are human beings, it may be argued that it is morally wrong to deny unborn human beings the status of personhood. If it is accepted, as I believe, that the unborn members of the human species are human beings, then it is arguable that as human beings they are natural persons as a matter of law. If all this is true, I contend that it is immoral and legally wrong to exclude the unborn human being at any age prior to birth from the constitutional meaning of person under the Fourteenth Amendment to the U. S. Constitution. It is my position that American constitutional law will not conform to the rule of law, and will fail to honor the basic doctrines of

Charles I. Lugosi, "Conforming to the Law: When Person and Human Being Finally Mean the Same Thing in Fourteenth Amendment Jurisprudence," *Issues in Law and Medicine*, Fall 2006/Spring 2007. Reproduced by permission. www.encyclopedia.com/doc/1G1-157268685.html.

equal protection under the law and substantive human rights, until the legal meanings of "human being" and "person" are identical and are mutually recognized as a matter of constitutional law when a new human being is created at the time of conception.

Denial of constitutional personhood to the unborn human being segregates an entire class of the human family making the unborn human being legally separate and unequal to those members of the human family who have been born. The result is that only those wanted children who are chosen to live and who are in fact born become legally recognized as a person following a live birth. For it is birth that marks the current legal boundary when a legal person is recognized in the United States of America, and bestows the constitutional rights of life, liberty and citizenship. . . .

As a matter of current American constitutional law, the word "person" does not have the same meaning as "human being," until the process of live birth has been completed. Until then, the law permits parents, doctors, scientists, and judges, amongst others, to openly discriminate between human beings that are chosen for birth and those that are not. Even though in the United States, the Fourteenth Amendment to the Constitution offers a right of equal protection and due process so that no person is deprived of his or her life or liberty, this right is denied to any human being who is not defined as a person—all unborn human beings.

I contend that the Fourteenth Amendment, unlike the Fifth Amendment, which was intended to protect people from government, was intended to protect people from discrimination and harm from other people. Racism is not the only thing people need protection from. As a living constitutional principle, the Fourteenth Amendment is not confined to its historical origin and purpose, but is available now to protect all human beings that are defined as non-persons, including all unborn human beings, individually, and as a class. The Su-

*Anti-abortion protestors march in front of the United States Supreme Court on January 22, 1996, the 23rd anniversary of* Roe v. Wade. Reuters/Bruce Young/Archive Photos, Inc. Reproduced by permission.

preme Court can define "person" to include all human beings, born and unborn. It simply chooses not to do so. It is a matter of judicial interpretation. . . .

## All Persons, Born and Unborn, Have a Right to Equal Protection

I maintain that there is no rule of law if the Constitution is interpreted to perpetuate a legal caste system of "separate and unequal," where there is no justice for the unborn. I contend there is no justice for the unborn human being so long as there is denial of equality, respect, dignity, liberty, life, and due process of law. Since the word "person" in the Fourteenth Amendment is capable of being interpreted liberally in an objective manner consistent with the rule of law to include all human beings, not to do so violates the natural law which is the foundation of the Declaration of Independence and the core liberal ideals of equality and human dignity.

Finally, I will argue that all unborn human beings, whether wanted or not, have a right to equal protection and due process under the Fourteenth Amendment. If I am right, then the Constitution gives all embryos and fetuses the right to life and the inherent right to be born, free from the current and future threats of unnatural death and involuntary sacrificial exploitation as subjects in medical experiments.

Relying on the reasoning of the Supreme Court in *Brown v. Board of Education*, . . . the U.S. Supreme Court can overrule *Roe v. Wade* on the grounds of equal protection alone. Such a result would not return the matter of abortion to the various states. The Fourteenth Amendment would thereafter prohibit abortion in every state. . . .

Does the word "person" in the Fourteenth Amendment include unborn human beings? If it does, then embryonic stem cell research, cloning, the destruction of IVF embryos, and abortion are potentially unlawful. If it does not, as a matter of logic and consistency, cloning, embryonic stem cell research, the freezing and destruction of embryos, and abortions ought all to be lawful, subject to rational regulation. . . .

It is not the role of the state government to protect pregnant women from alleged private violence represented by the biological condition of pregnancy. Even if it can be successfully argued that pregnancy must be consensual for it to be permitted to continue, the *DeShaney* case [*DeShaney v. Winnebago County*] has closed the door to any substantive due process claim that pregnant women are constitutionally entitled to rely on the state to protect them from private violence within their womb.

The reality is that pregnancy is not a criminal assault, and therefore is not a crime. Normally pregnancy is not a disease either, for it is the reproductive phase in the life of a healthy expectant mother. Pregnancy is a naturally occurring physical condition that is normal, for reproduction is integral to the human condition and essential to the survival of humanity.

If there is any future potential for advancing the case for abortion, it may perhaps be found in the difference between the constitutional status of a person and a citizen. Birth still marks the boundary when an unborn person acquires the privileges and immunities of a citizen. Unborn persons are still not citizens, for only born or naturalized persons qualify for citizenship, and all the privileges and immunities that attach to that status.

In the meantime, by virtue of the Equal Protection Clause of the Fourteenth Amendment, the unborn person will have a superior claim to life over any existing moral or jurisprudential argument in favor of abortion.

# Appendices

# Appendix A

## The Amendments to the U.S. Constitution

Amendment I:      Freedom of Religion, Speech, Press, Petition, and
                  Assembly (ratified 1791)

Amendment II:     Right to Bear Arms (ratified 1791)

Amendment III:    Quartering of Soldiers (ratified 1791)

Amendment IV:     Freedom from Unfair Search and Seizures
                  (ratified 1791)

Amendment V:      Right to Due Process (ratified 1791)

Amendment VI:     Rights of the Accused (ratified 1791)

Amendment VII:    Right to Trial by Jury (ratified 1791)

Amendment VIII:   Freedom from Cruel and Unusual Punishment
                  (ratified 1791)

Amendment IX:     Construction of the Constitution (ratified 1791)

Amendment X:      Powers of the States and People (ratified 1791)

Amendment XI:     Judicial Limits (ratified 1795)

Amendment XII:    Presidential Election Process (ratified 1804)

Amendment XIII:   Abolishing Slavery (ratified 1865)

Amendment XIV:    Equal Protection, Due Process, Citizenship for All
                  (ratified 1868)

# The Amendments to the U.S. Constitution

Amendment XV:    Race and the Right to Vote (ratified 1870)

Amendment XVI:    Allowing Federal Income Tax (ratified 1913)

Amendment XVII:    Establishing Election to the U.S. Senate (ratified 1913)

Amendment XVIII:    Prohibition (ratified 1919)

Amendment XIX:    Granting Women the Right to Vote (ratified 1920)

Amendment XX:    Establishing Term Commencement for Congress and the President (ratified 1933)

Amendment XXI:    Repeal of Prohibition (ratified 1933)

Amendment XXII:    Establishing Term Limits for U.S. President (ratified 1951)

Amendment XXIII:    Allowing Washington, D.C., Representation in the Electoral College (ratified 1961)

Amendment XXIV:    Prohibition of the Poll Tax (ratified 1964)

Amendment XXV:    Presidential Disability and Succession (ratified 1967)

Amendment XXVI:    Lowering the Voting Age (ratified 1971)

Amendment XXVII:    Limiting Congressional Pay Increases (ratified 1992)

# Appendix B

## Court Cases Relevant to the Fourteenth Amendment's Equal Protection Clause

### Slaughterhouse Cases, 1873
The Supreme Court interpreted the Fourteenth Amendment for the first time and ruled, among other things, that it was intended only to protect the rights of former slaves, disallowing a broader interpretation.

### *Strauder v. West Virginia,* 1880
The Supreme Court ruled that to exclude blacks from juries violates the equal protection right of black criminal defendants.

### Civil Rights Cases, 1883
The Supreme Court ruled that the Civil Rights Act of 1875 was unconstitutional because the Fourteenth Amendment prohibits discrimination by states, not individuals, and Congress has no power to regulate the conduct of private companies.

### *Pace v. Alabama,* 1883
The Supreme Court ruled that anti-miscegenation laws (laws against sex between members of different races) did not violate the Equal Protection Clause. This decision was overturned in 1964 by *McLaughlin v. Florida* and in 1967 by *Loving v. Virginia.*

### *Yick Wo v. Hopkins,* 1886
For the first time applying the Equal Protection Clause to a minority other than blacks, the Supreme Court ruled that laws which in effect discriminate against a particular group—in this case, the Chinese—are unconstitutional.

*Plessy v. Ferguson,* **1896**
The Supreme Court ruled that racial segregation was constitutional, thus establishing the "separate but equal" doctrine that remained in effect for more than half a century.

*Williams v. Mississippi,* **1898**
The Supreme Court ruled that a poll tax and literacy requirements that prevented blacks from voting did not violate the Equal Protection Clause because in theory they applied to all voters, even though illiterate whites were exempted under a "grandfather" clause.

*Cumming v. Richmond County Board of Education,* **1899**
The Supreme Court ruled that a city tax that supported only white schools did not violate the Equal Protection Clause. This decision was overturned in 1954 by *Brown v. Board of Education.*

*Buchanan v. Warley,* **1917**
The Supreme Court ruled that zoning laws requiring residential segregation based on race violate the Equal Protection Clause.

*Gitlow v. New York,* **1925**
The Supreme Court ruled that the Fourteenth Amendment extends some provisions of the Bill of Rights—freedom speech and freedom of the press—to state governments.

*Lum v. Rice,* **1927**
The Supreme Court ruled that Chinese children could be excluded from white schools.

*Nixon v. Herndon,* **1927**
The Supreme Court ruled that a Texas law under which blacks were not allowed to vote in the Democratic Party primary violated the Equal Protection Clause.

*Nixon v. Condon,* **1932**
After the *Nixon v. Herndon* decision, Texas changed its law to say that political parties could determine in their own way who could vote in their primaries, and Nixon, who was black,

still was not allowed to vote. The Supreme Court ruled that although parties are private organizations, because the Democratic party was acting under a state grant of power it was subject to the Fourteenth Amendment, and therefore it could not deny equal protection to blacks.

### Norris v. Alabama, 1935
The Supreme Court ruled that to exclude blacks from a jury on the basis of their race violates the Equal Protection Clause.

### Missouri ex rel. Gaines v. Canada, 1938
In the first case in which it considered equality of education for blacks, the Supreme Court ruled that if a state provides legal education to white students, it must also provide it to black students.

### United States v. Carolene Products, 1938
Although this is not a Fourteenth Amendment case, it is significant because in a famous footnote to its opinion, the Supreme Court first proposed the idea of requiring different levels of scrutiny for different types of equal protection cases.

### Skinner v. Oklahoma, 1942
The Supreme Court ruled that compulsory sterilization as a punishment for crime violates the Equal Protection Clause if it is applied only to certain categories of crimes.

### Smith v. Allwright, 1944
The Supreme Court ruled that although political parties are private organizations not normally covered by the Fourteenth Amendment, people cannot be excluded from them on the basis of race.

### Oyama v. State of California, 1948
The Supreme Court ruled that certain provisions of California's Alien Land Laws, which barred persons ineligible to become citizens from owning land, denied equal protection of the law to the U.S. born children of Japanese parents who, being themselves unable to buy land, attempted to purchase it in their children's name.

### Shelley v. Kraemer, 1948
The Supreme Court ruled that although racially based restrictions on ownership of private property are not banned under the Fourteenth Amendment, they cannot be legally enforced because state action to enforce them would violate the Equal Protection Clause.

### Sipuel v. Board of Regents of University of Oklahoma, 1948
The Supreme Court ruled that under the Equal Protection Clause, colleges cannot deny admittance to students on the basis of race.

### McLaurin v. Oklahoma State Regents, 1950
The Supreme Court ruled that it is a violation of the Equal Protection Clause for a public institution of higher learning to treat a student differently from other students solely because of his or her race.

### Sweatt v. Painter, 1950
The Supreme Court ruled that the Equal Protection Clause requires that at the graduate level, educational opportunities available to blacks and whites must be of equal quality.

### Brown v. Board of Education, 1954
The Supreme Court overturned *Plessy v. Ferguson* by ruling that racial segregation in public schools is unconstitutional under the Equal Protection Clause.

### Bolling v. Sharpe, 1954
In an influential case that established the relevance of the Equal Protection Clause to federal laws, the Supreme Court ruled that although the Fourteenth Amendment does not apply to the District of Columbia, it is unconstitutional under the Fifth Amendment (which refers only to due process) for its schools to be segregated by race, because "discrimination may be so unjustifiable as to be violative of due process."

### Burton v. Wilmington Parking Authority, 1961
The Supreme Court ruled that it is a violation of the Equal Protection Clause for a restaurant located in a public parking building to discriminate on the basis of race, even though the restaurant itself is privately operated.

### Baker v. Carr, 1962

The Supreme Court ruled that it is a violation of the Equal Protection Clause for lines between voting districts to be drawn in a way that gives some districts more people than others, thus making urban citizens' votes worth less than those of rural citizens.

### Gray v. Sanders, 1963

The Supreme Court ruled that voting systems that treat counties as units violate the Equal Protection Clause because they cause the votes of people in small counties to be worth more than those of people in large counties.

### McLaughlin v. Florida, 1964

The Supreme Court ruled that laws that bar unmarried couples of different races from living together, but do not apply to unmarried couples of the same race, violate the Equal Protection Clause.

### Reynolds v. Sims, 1964

The Supreme Court ruled that the Equal Protection Clause requires state legislature districts to be roughly equal in population.

### Wesberry v. Sanders, 1964

The Supreme Court ruled that the Equal Protection Clause requires congressional districts to be roughly equal in population.

### Baxstrom v. Herold, 1966

The Supreme Court ruled that it is a violation of the Equal Protection Clause for a mentally ill prisoner to be civilly committed to a hospital after completion of his prison sentence without the judicial determination of dangerousness required for others who are committed.

### Harper v. Virginia Board Of Elections, 1966

The Supreme Court ruled that for a state to make voting conditional on payment of a poll tax violates the Equal Protection Clause.

## *Loving v. Virginia,* 1967

The Supreme Court ruled that under the Equal Protection Clause, laws against interracial marriage are unconstitutional.

## *Avery v. Midland County,* 1968

In a case similar to *Reynolds v. Sims,* the Supreme Court held that the principle of comparable population in voting districts also applies to local government.

## *Kramer v. Union School District,* 1969

The Supreme Court ruled that to require that citizens either own property in a school district or be parents or guardians of school-age children in order to vote in that district's elections is a unreasonable restriction of the right to vote.

## *Dandridge v. Williams,* 1970

The Supreme Court ruled that for a state to put a ceiling on grants to families under the Aid to Families with Dependent Children program does not violate the Equal Protection Clause even though it may not meet the need of especially large families.

## *Coit v. Green,* 1971

The Supreme Court ruled that using federal funds to finance private schools that are racially segregated violates the Equal Protection Clause.

## *Palmer v. Thompson,* 1971

The Supreme Court ruled that it is not a violation of the Equal Protection Clause for a city to shut down its swimming pools in order to avoid racial integration.

## *Pennsylvania Association of Retarded Children v. Commonwealth of Pennsylvania,* 1971

The Supreme Court ruled that the Equal Protection Clause requires states to provide education for developmentally disabled children.

## Reed v. Reed, 1971
In the first Supreme Court case in which the Equal Protection Clause was used to establish the rights of women, the Court ruled that men cannot be automatically preferred over women as administrators of estates.

## Swann v. Charlotte-Mecklenburg County Board of Education, 1971
The Supreme Court affirmed busing as a means of achieving school desegregation and ruled that the existence of all-black or all-white schools, even if based on residence of students, must be shown not to be due to segregation.

## Eisenstadt v. Baird, 1972
The Supreme Court ruled that laws prohibiting the distribution of contraceptives to unmarried people, but not to married people, violate the Equal Protection Clause.

## Stanley v. Illinois, 1972
The Supreme Court ruled that because a married father would have custody of his child upon the mother's death, it is a violation of the Equal Protection Clause for an unmarried father who has a relationship with his child not to receive a hearing as to his parental fitness before the state can take custody.

## San Antonio School District v. Rodriguez, 1973
The Supreme Court ruled that basing school financing on property taxes does not violate the Equal Protection Clause even when it causes disparities in education between school districts.

## Benner v. Oswald, 1974
The Supreme Court ruled that the Equal Protection Clause does not require that undergraduate students be allowed to participate in the selection of a university's board of trustees.

## Geduldig v. Aiello, 1974
The Supreme Court ruled that the denial of insurance benefits for work loss resulting from a normal pregnancy did not violate the Equal Protection Clause because it distinguished not between women and men, but between pregnant women and everybody else, male or female.

### Kahn v. Shevin, 1974

The Supreme Court ruled that a Florida state law giving a property tax exemption to widows, but not widowers, had a rational basis because financial difficulties of women were greater than those of men, and that it therefore did not violate the Equal Protection Clause.

### Milliken v. Bradley, 1974

The Supreme Court ruled that the Constitution does not require busing from one school district to another in order to achieve racial balance in schools unless there is evidence that the school districts involved had deliberately engaged in segregation.

### Richardson v. Ramirez, 1974

The Supreme Court ruled that it is not a violation of the Equal Protection Clause for convicted felons to be denied the right to vote.

### Stanton v. Stanton, 1975

The Supreme Court ruled that laws setting different ages of majority for men and women violate the Equal Protection Clause.

### Craig v. Boren, 1976

The Supreme Court ruled for the first time that laws which classify people by gender must be subjected to "intermediate scrutiny," meaning that a law is unconstitutional under the Equal Protection Clause unless it is "substantially related" to an "important" government interest.

### New Orleans v. Dukes, 1976

The Supreme Court ruled that it was not a violation of the Equal Protection Clause for a city to ban pushcart vendors who had operated for less than the number of years specified in a "grandfather" clause.

### Washington v. Davis, 1976

In a case involving alleged discrimination in the hiring of Washington, D.C. police officers, the Supreme Court ruled that for an action to be unconstitutional under the Equal Protection Clause, there must be discriminatory intent, rather than just a racially disparate result.

### Regents of the University of California v. Bakke, 1978
The Supreme Court ruled that racial quotas cannot not be used in determining college admissions, but that race can be used as a factor in individual cases.

### Orr v. Orr, 1979
In a decision that altered the legal basis of marriage, the Supreme Court ruled that state laws providing that husbands, but not wives, might be required to pay alimony after a divorce are unconstitutional under the Equal Protection Clause.

### Mississippi University for Women v. Hogan, 1982
The Supreme Court ruled that for a university to deny otherwise qualified males the right to enroll for credit in its School of Nursing violates the Equal Protection Clause.

### Michael M. v. Superior Court of Sonoma County, 1981
The Supreme Court upheld California's statutory rape law, under which, in a case of consensual sex between a couple under 18, the male was guilty of a crime while the female was not. It ruled that this was not a violation of equal protection because men and women are not similarly situated with regard to the burdens of teenage pregnancy.

### Plyler v. Doe, 1982
The Supreme Court ruled that the Fourteenth Amendment applies to all persons who reside in a state whether or not they are citizens and that the children of illegal immigrants therefore have a right to the same free education given other children.

### Bernal v. Fainter, 1984
The Supreme Court ruled that the Equal Protection Clause prohibits barring a noncitizen from applying for commission as a notary public.

## City of Cleburne v. Cleburne Living Center, 1985
The Supreme Court ruled that denial of building permits to homes for the mentally retarded is discriminatory and therefore unconstitutional.

## Hooper v. Bernalillo County Assessor, 1985
The Supreme Court ruled that a past residence requirement in a New Mexico property tax exemption for Vietnam war veterans violated the Equal Protection Clause.

## Batson v. Kentucky, 1986
The Supreme Court ruled that prosecutors cannot make preemptory challenges (exclude jurors without stating a valid cause) solely on the basis of race.

## Davis v. Bandemer, 1986
The Supreme Court ruled that partisan gerrymandering (setting district boundaries so as to give the opposing political party a majority in as few districts as possible) violates the Equal Protection Clause if, and only if, certain conditions exist.

## Richmond v. J.A. Croson Co, 1989
The Supreme Court ruled that giving preference to minority business enterprises in the awarding of municipal contracts is unconstitutional under the Equal Protection Clause.

## Gregory v. Ashcroft, 1991
The Supreme Court ruled that for a state to have a mandatory retirement age for judges is not a violation of the Equal Protection Clause.

## Hernandez v. New York, 1991
The Supreme Court ruled that it is not a violation of the Equal Protection Clause to exclude bilingual persons from a jury on the grounds that they will be unable to limit their understanding of Spanish testimony to what is in the official translation.

### Powers v. Ohio, 1991

The Supreme Court ruled that under the Equal Protection Clause, a criminal defendant may object to race-based exclusions of jurors through peremptory challenges whether or not the defendant and the excluded jurors share the same race.

### Georgia v. McCollum, 1992

The Supreme Court ruled that a criminal defendant cannot make preemptory challenges (exclude jurors without stating a valid cause) solely on the basis of race.

### Shaw v. Reno, 1993

The Supreme Court ruled that arranging the boundaries of electoral districts in order to create minority majorities and thus elect more minority representatives to Congress is a violation of the Equal Protection Clause.

### J.E.B. v. Alabama, 1994

The Supreme Court ruled that preemptory challenges cannot be made solely on the basis of a prospective juror's gender.

### Miller v. Johnson, 1995

The Supreme Court ruled that boundaries of electoral districts cannot be set in such a way as to purposely create minority majorities.

### Hopwood v. Texas, 1996

The Supreme Court ruled that reverse discrimination (the favoring of black students over white students) in law school admissions violates the Equal Protection Clause. This decision was overturned in 2003 by *Grutter v. Bollinger*.

### Romer v. Evans, 1996

The Supreme Court ruled that under the Equal Protection Clause, states cannot prohibit local governments from passing ordinances to protect homosexuals from discrimination.

### United States v. Virginia, 1996

The Supreme Court ruled that for admission to a publicly supported school or college to be restricted by gender violates the Equal Protection Clause.

### Vacco v. Quill, 1997

The Supreme Court ruled that New York's ban on physician-assisted suicide did not violate the Equal Protection Clause in allowing competent terminally ill adults to hasten their own death by refusing lifesaving treatment, but denying that right to patients for whom withdrawal of treatment would not hasten death.

### Bush v. Gore, 2000

The Supreme Court ruled that because Florida's method of recounting ballots was inconsistent between counties, it did not provide voters with equal protection under the law, and that the recount must therefore be stopped. This determined the outcome of the presidential election.

### Kimel v. Florida Board of Regents, 2000

In a case involving the Age Discrimination in Employment Act (ADEA), the Supreme Count ruled that where discrimination has a rational basis, the federal government's power to enforce the Fourteenth Amendment does not override the principle that individuals cannot sue state governments.

### Village of Willowbrook v. Olech, 2001

The Supreme Court ruled that an equal protection claim can brought by a single individual alleging arbitrary treatment at the hands of a local government. This was an influential decision because previous equal protection cases were based on membership in classes of citizens who were discriminated against; here the Court authorized "class-of-one" claims.

### Fitzgerald v. Racing Association of Central Iowa, 2003

The Supreme Court ruled that for a state to levy different tax rates against racetrack and casino gambling does not violate the Equal Protection Clause because there may be a rational basis for the difference.

### Gratz v. Bollinger, 2003

In a case where white students were denied admission to a university because blacks were given an advantage solely on the basis of race, the Supreme Court ruled that use of an arbitrary point system to choose among applicants is unconstitutional under the Equal Protection Clause.

### *Grutter v. Bollinger,* 2003
The Supreme Court ruled that using race as a factor in college admissions does not violate the constitutional right to equal protection if the policy is "narrowly tailored" to achieve racial diversity among the student body and the selection is made on an individual basis.

### *Lawrence v. Texas,* 2003
The Supreme Court struck down state laws banning sex between consenting same-sex adults. Although the petitioners in this case argued that such laws violated both the Equal Protection Clause and the Due Process Clause of the Fourteenth Amendment, the Court's majority opinion was based only on the Due Process Clause.

### *Halbert v. Michigan,* 2005
The Supreme Court ruled that the Equal Protection and Due Process Clauses require the appointment of counsel for defendants convicted on their pleas who wish to take their cases to an appellate court.

### *Parents v. Seattle,* 2007
The Supreme Court ruled that it is a violation of the Equal Protection Clause to use race as an arbitrary factor in assigning students to schools, even if the purpose is to maintain racial diversity.

# For Further Research

## Books

Angelo N. Ancheta, *Scientific Evidence and Equal Protection of the Law*. New Brunswick, NJ: Rutgers University Press, 2006.

Judith A. Baer, *Equality Under the Constitution: Reclaiming the Fourteenth Amendment*. Ithaca, NY: Cornell University Press, 1983.

Raoul Berger, *The Fourteenth Amendment and the Bill of Rights*. Norman: University of Oklahoma Press, 1989.

———, *Government by Judiciary: The Transformation of the Fourteenth Amendment*. Indianapolis, IN: Liberty Fund, 1997.

James E. Bond, *No Easy Walk to Freedom: Reconstruction and the Ratification of the Fourteenth Amendment*. Westport, CN: Praeger, 1997.

Anthony Cortese, *Opposing Hate Speech*, Westport, CN: Praeger, 2006.

Michael Kent Curtis, *No State Shall Abridge: The Fourteenth Amendment and the Bill of Rights*. Durham, NC: Duke University Press, 1990.

Garrett Epps, *Democracy Reborn: The Fourteenth Amendment and the Fight for Equal Rights in Post–Civil War America*. New York: Henry Holt, 2006.

Harvey Fireside, *Separate and Unequal: Homer Plessy and the Supreme Court Decision That Legalized Racism*. New York: Carroll and Graf, 2004.

Horace Edgar Flack, *Adoption of the Fourteenth Amendment*. Buffalo, NY: W.S. Hein, 2003.

Eric Foner, *Reconstruction: America's Unfinished Revolution, 1863–1877.* New York: Perennial Classics, 2002.

Evan Gerstmann, *The Constitutional Underclass: Gays, Lesbians, and the Failure of Class-Based Equal Protection.* Chicago: University of Chicago Press, 1999.

Robert P. Green, ed., *Equal Protection and the African American Constitutional Experience: A Documentary History.* Westport, CN: Greenwood Press, 2000.

Joseph B. James, *The Ratification of the Fourteenth Amendment.* Macon, GA: Mercer University Press, 1984.

Kenneth L. Karst, *Belonging to America: Equal Citizenship and the Constitution.* New Haven, CT: Yale University Press, 1989.

Michael J. Klarman, *From Jim Crow to Civil Rights: The Supreme Court and the Struggle for Racial Equality.* New York: Oxford University Press, 2004.

Ronald M. Labbé and Jonathan Lurie, *The Slaughterhouse Cases: Regulation, Reconstruction, and the Fourteenth Amendment.* Abridged Edition. Lawrence: University Press of Kansas, 2005.

Darien A. McWhirter, *Equal Protection.* Phoenix, AZ: Oryx Press, 1995.

Howard N. Meyer, *The Amendment that Refused to Die: Equality and Justice Deferred: The History of the Fourteenth Amendment.* Lanham, MD: Madison Books, 2000.

Joyce Murdoch and Deb Price, *Courting Justice: Gay Men and Lesbians v. the Supreme Court.* New York: Basic Books, 2001.

William E. Nelson, *The Fourteenth Amendment: From Political Principle to Judicial Doctrine.* Cambridge, MA: Harvard University Press, 1988.

James T. Patterson, *Brown v. Board of Education: A Civil Rights Milestone and Its Troubled Legacy.* New York: Oxford University Press, 2001.

Michael J. Perry, *We the People: The Fourteenth Amendment and the Supreme Court.* New York: Oxford University Press, 1999.

## Periodicals

Robert J. Bresler, "The Supreme Court 'Races' On," *USA Today Magazine*, September 1, 2007.

Curtis Crawford, "Racial Preference Versus Nondiscrimination," *Society*, March/April 2004.

Michael Daniel, "Using the Fourteenth Amendment to Improve Environmental Justice," *Human Rights*, vol. 30, no. 4, Fall 2003.

Edwin C. Darden, "The Diversity Test," *American School Board Journal*, vol. 8, no. 4, October 2006.

Paul Finkelman, "John Bingham and the Background to the Fourteenth Amendment," *Akron Law Review*, vol. 36, no. 4, 2003.

Stanley Fish, "History, Principle, and Affirmative Action," *New York Times*, July 14, 2007.

Eric Foner and Randall Kennedy, "Brown at 50," *Nation*, May 3, 2004.

Steven Geoffrey Gieseler, "Equal Protection vs. Equal Results," *Washington Times*, May 4, 2008.

Linda Greenhouse, "Justices Reject 'Class of One' Argument," *New York Times*, June 10, 2008.

Harriet McBryde Johnson, "The Way We Live Now: 5-30-04; Stairway to Justice," *New York Times Magazine*, May 30, 2004.

Gerald S. McCorkle, "Busing Comes to Dallas Schools," *Southwestern Historical Quarterly*, vol. 111, no. 3, January 2008.

Ramesh Ponnuru, "Originalist Sin: Conservatives, the Constitution, and Affirmative Action," *National Review*, March 10, 2003.

Thomas Sowell, "Justice Kennedy's New Move Left: Soft on Crime," *Human Events*, August 18, 2003.

Joseph Summerill, "Supreme Court Rules that Racially Segregating Inmates Is Unconstitutional," *Corrections Today*, June 1, 2005.

Amy Stuart Wells and Erica Frankenberg, "The Public Schools and the Challenge of the Supreme Court's Integration Decision," *Phi Delta Kappan*, vol. 89, no. 3, November 2007.

Barry Yeoman, "When Is a Corporation Like a Freed Slave?," *Mother Jones*, November/December 2006.

Robert Zelnick, "Confronting Affirmative Action," *National Review*, August 9, 2004.

Rebecca E. Zietlow, "Congressional Enforcement of Civil Rights and John Bingham's Theory of Citizenship," *Akron Law Review*, vol. 36, no. 4, 2003.

## Internet Sources

Barbara Belejack, "A Lesson in Equal Protection," *Texas Observer*, July 13, 2007. www.texasobserver.org.

Cheryl A. Brooks, "Politics of Forgetting: How Oregon Forgot to Ratify the Fourteenth Amendment," *Oregon Humanities*, Fall/Winter 2006. www.oregonhum.org.

Roger Clegg and Keith Noreika, "Racial Profiling, Equal Protection, and the War Against Terrorism," Federalist Society, December 1, 2003. www.fed-soc.org.

Cornell University Law School, *Equal Protection: An Overview*, n.d. www.law.cornell.edu.

Clare Cushman, ed., "Supreme Court Decisions and Women's Rights: Milestones to Equality," Supreme Court Historical Society, 2000. www.supremecourthistory.org.

Eric Foner, "The Reconstruction Amendments: Official Documents as Social History," *History Now Online*, December 2004. www.historynow.org.

Harry V. Jaffa, "The Logic of the Colorblind Constitution," Claremont Institute, December 6, 2004. www.claremont .org.

Nicholas Jenkins, "Gay Marriages Would Violate Equal Protection," *Intellectual Conservative*, November 25, 2003. www.intellectualconservative.com.

Doug Kendall, "Constitutionally Incorrect," *New Republic*, March 26, 2008. www.tnr.com.

Anne P. Mitchell, "Equal Protection Under the Law?" Separated Parenting Access & Resource Center, n.d. www.deltabravo.net.

Peter Namtvedt, "Equal Protection of the Laws," *From Reason to Freedom*, October 10, 2007. www.reasontofreedom.com.

Amy Ridenour, "Equal Protection Under the Law: Is Andrew Sullivan Right About Gay Marriage?" National Center for Public Policy Research, February 2004. www.national center.org.

U.S. Department of State, *Equal Protection of the Law*, June 23, 2008. www.america.gov.

Women's Justice Center, *The Maria Teresa Macias Case: The Fourteenth Amendment, for Women?* 2002. www.justice women.com.

# Web Sites

**Constitutional Rights Foundation**, www.crf-usa.org. Detailed material on various constitutional rights issues, including a number of current equal protection topics.

**Library of Congress Web Guides: Primary Documents in American History: 14th Amendment to the U.S. Constitution**, www.loc.gov. Links to primary documents and other relevant sites.

# Index

Voting rights
  for blacks, 20
  political parties and, 29

# W

*Wade, Roe v.*, 180, 184, 189
*Warley, Buchanan v.*, 195
Warren, Earl, 92, 148, 157
Warren Court, 148
*Washington v. Davis*, 201–202
Weddington, Sarah, 184
*Wesberry v. Sanders*, 198
*West Virginia, Strauder v.*, 28, 194
Wildmon, Don, 176
*Williams, Dandridge v.*, 199
*Williams v. Mississippi*, 195
*Wilmington Parking Authority, Burton v.*, 197

Wilson, Henry, 64, *66*
*Winnebago County, DeShaney v.*, 181, 189
*Wisconsin v. Yoder*, 121
Women
  consent to pregnancy by, 180–185
  discrimination against, 112–115
  rights of, 21, 23, 30

# Y

*Yick Wo v. Hopkins*, 23, 28, 73–78, 117–118, 194
*Yoder, Wisconsin v.*, 121

# Z

Zorn, Eric, 174–175